WIN FRIENDS,
PEOPLE AND C

PREPARE
PERSUADE
CONQUER

MICHAEL LEE

Praise for Michael Lee

From: Dr. Joe Rubino,
Creator of *lifeoptimizationcoaching.com* *and* *theselfesteembook.com*

I love this book! It's fun to read, reveals powerful info straight to you and gives plenty of examples so you can quickly understand how to apply the info in the real world.

My favorite part is the "Prepare" chapters, where Michael shows you how to alter your belief and acquire the mindset of a master persuader.

After all, you won't succeed using ANY persuasion technique until you really believe you can persuade. His 5-step preparation system, as well as his solutions to possible obstacles, are sheer genius.

Read this book, you'll thank me later!

From: Mason Ramm
www.LittleKnownWaysToMakeMoney.com from Brisbane, Australia

Persuasion has always fascinated me. But after reading many materials on the subject, I still can't persuade people in real life. After reading just Chapter 1 of "Prepare, Persuade, Conquer," I finally GOT IT!

I found the reason why I can't persuade before, and the ultimate solution to start persuading successfully from then on. I was able to 'program' myself to take in the qualities of a master persuader. I'm now able to persuade others more than ever.

Not only that, Technique # 5 of Chapter 1 has allowed me to acquire almost any trait or emotion I desire - whether it's to become happier, more motivated, more confident, etc.

If Chapter 1 has just changed my life, I wonder what amazing success awaits me after reading the whole book!

From: Richard Quek
www.richardquek.com from Selangor, Malaysia

As a network marketer and internet marketer, knowing how to sell and build relationships is a necessity. "Prepare, Persuade, Conquer" has helped me tremendously in those areas.

Michael's 5 masterful steps in selling have increased my profits, while his 10 ways to "make people like you" has allowed me to gain trust and respect from everyone.

Although the techniques are very simple to apply, they are also very effective. Thanks, Michael.

From: Alfonso Roy Alvin C. Montenegro
Leyte, Philippines

I love Michael Lee's extensive knowledge in the art of persuasion. Not only is his writing style very personal, but it is very easy to understand. You can really tell that he practices what he preaches.

I started using one technique in "Prepare, Persuade, Conquer" about how to diffuse criticism and it worked like a charm! I realized that I used it when I was young and I wasn't aware that it was such a powerful technique.

I taught it to my nephew and it has become his favorite weapon against people who have nothing good to say to him. I watched how he used it in action; and boy, it was so fun seeing how he disarmed the person who criticized him.

Read this book. It will help you succeed in life faster than you ever thought possible!

From: Jones Mancilla
Online Team Strategist of PositivelyAwesomeVA.com

You can immediately practice Michael's persuasion tactics within 20 seconds of reading... even if you are shy, an introvert, have very limited friends and very soft spoken.

The persuasion tactics - specifically the right mindset, right affirmations and how to manage objections - have helped me transition in my career and get long-term clients for my online business.

From: John Vincent
www.JohnVincent.tv from Henley on Thames, UK

No Fluff or filler here! This book reminded me of lots of things I've learned in seminars around the world as well as giving practical real world examples of how to use them.

The Zeigarnik effect (something that was new to me) has already helped me create a compelling new video that I know is going to make a huge difference to my results.

This book covers so much ground that if you only implement 10% of it you will reap many times the value of your investment! Get a massive advantage and use this information to make your life and that of the people around you a better place.

From: Alan Tutt
www.PowerKeysPub.com, Photographer, Author, &
Publisher

Hi Michael,

I want to thank you for writing "Prepare, Persuade, & Conquer." As a student of psychology and persuasion, I thought I knew everything there was to know about the subject. However, the more I read your new book, the more I learned.

Chapter 10 was especially enlightening. While many folks talk about the power of reciprocity, you made it clear how most use it incorrectly, and how to best use it without being manipulative.

Chapter 13 covers a topic I know intimately, and it works exactly as you say it does. As a photographer taking photos of school children for yearbooks, I can report that their actions often do reflect the photographer's expectations.

From: Karl Moore
www.karlmoore.com, best-selling author and entrepreneur

Michael is a genius!

In this book, he's taken the best techniques from an entire industry, and crystallized them down into quick, easy-to-digest chapters.

Unlike most books out there, there is zero padding inside 'Prepare,
Persuade, Conquer.' Instead, it's crammed with actionable content that can bring real change and success to your life.

From: Natalie Ledwell
www.mindmovies.com

'Prepare Persuade Conquer' is a brilliant work of art in the area of persuasion. I love the way it teaches you how to rewire your mind and prepare you to become a master persuader.

The secrets and techniques are unique and well-explained... with practical examples to show you how to apply them in the real world. Another thing I love about this book is the summary outline that lists down the key points to remember.

This amazing book is worth much, much more than the price it's selling for.

Please feel free to send me an email. Just know that these emails are filtered by my publisher. Good news is always welcome.

Michael Lee - **michael_lee@awesomeauthors.org**

Check out my site for free gifts, updates, and interesting info:
www.expertpersuader.com

About the Publisher

BLVNP Incorporated, A Nevada Corporation, 340 S. Lemon #6200, Walnut CA 91789, info@blvnp.com / legal@blvnp.com

DISCLAIMER

PREPARE
PERSUADE
CONQUER
**Win Friends, Influence People
and Get the Yes**

By: Michael Lee

©Michael Lee 2014
ISBN: 978-1-68030-906-5

TABLE OF CONTENTS

FOREWORD

By: Kevin Hogan[1]

Persuasion...

"It's manipulation."
"It can be used for evil."
"It is used to control people."

These are the comments and press conference-related questions I hear all around the world.

This means there is a big, overwhelming gap between what effective persuasion and communication is.

Think about that last time you heard ANY communication that was NOT persuasive in nature in some way.

Perhaps someone over there smiles and says, "I'm not persuading when I say, 'I love you.'"

If that's true, then you are sending a mixed message. With every effective "I love you" comes the parallel message, "I want you to believe this is absolutely true."

When a child is on the street and you see a teenager driving a car 200 feet away with tunes blasting while he's texting his girlfriend, you have one chance—only one—to save the child's life. The driver sees no cars in front of him. The child on the street is not going to survive another 20 seconds unless...

---

[1] Author of "The Science of Influence" and "Invisible Influence" from Minneapolis, Minnesota

"Chrissy, come here, right NOW."

Because some people will say, "Honey, there is a car coming you should move out of the road."

Training people to respond to persuasive messages is more than important; it can save a life.

Saving lives...

When a medical doctor has a photograph of a patient in his file, the doctor does better work, identifies more problems in an MRI and helps the patient more. In fact, the results of studies in this area are so compelling there is no question that patients should REQUIRE their photographs to be part of their file.

Making lives better...

You can control differences in student performance. Let them take their college placement tests in smaller rooms, with smaller numbers of students taking the tests at smaller schools, and the students perform better. Significantly better.

You can take this one tiny fact of human influence further. Place the new male hire with a group of elite stars at the company and he will perform worse than if he begins with a few men who are just a little better at the job than he will shortly be. Meanwhile women will perform better if they work in elite environments.

Where you sit or stand is going to determine in significant terms, the results you are going to get when you present your proposal. Stand off to the left of who you are presenting to and you will lose sales you would have otherwise gotten. Stand off to their right and you will gain sales you would not have had a chance on.

How can that happen?

Because almost EVERYTHING influences the human brain or mind.

Things that affect the human mind, whether it's the color of the paint, the clothes you wear, the smile or lack of it you display, the car you drive up in or the person walking next to you, all increase or decrease the probabilities of influencing the person you are about to talk with.

More remarkably, the first story a person hears about you, true or false, proven true or false, dramatically influences how the person is going to feel about you minutes, hours, days and YEARS after you meet them.

Changing this initial impression is not impossible, but the initial impression has such a strong hold on how people decide that it requires enormous effort to overcome it.

You can lay out hundreds of pages of similar influences about what to do if you want your communication to be EFFECTIVE.

And that's what persuasion is. It's effective communication.

Every communication is a persuasive attempt.

The baby cries because she NEEDS SOMETHING. The baby is attempting to get mom or dad to help her and will continue to do so until she succeeds. Fortunately this was our first persuasive training so we all have SOME skill at getting what is important to us.

Unfortunately this is often where persuasive training stops.

To be sure, every communication is a persuasive attempt but most of them fail because they are impotent. You can cry and mom can trial-and-error her way to help, but when you learn to speak, that cry rarely has impact in most contexts.

Learning to persuade is learning to communicate effectively.

Truly brilliant communicators are rare. People don't take the time to learn to persuade so they live life insulting others by accident. They live a random life.

The Master of Persuasion has a purpose. The Master has considered outcomes and obstacles. The Master has given great thought to the client, to the girl he's going to ask out... and then ask to marry.

Michael Lee's new book is refreshing.

It's brief, simple, easy to apply and makes your life better.

How?

Through the science of persuasion.

Read it. Learn it. Drink it in.

It's not only a lot of fun, it's also a great read that you'll enjoy and use for the rest of your life.

Kevin Hogan
Author of "The Science of Influence" and "Invisible Influence"
Minneapolis, Minnesota

INTRODUCTION

It's been said that all problems in life are derived from only three sources – relationships, finances, and health. Although there are several ways to build fulfilling relationships, amass an abundance of wealth and enjoy radiant health, there's one solution that caters to all three – and that is persuasion.

Think about it. If you know how to persuade people, you can change their behavior and mindset. Instead of arguing with your spouse and kids, you can convince them to do what you want – and they'll be happy to do it for you. Imagine if you can influence your parents, relatives, or friends to your way of thinking without a hint of resistance; you'll feel more in control of your life! And if it's romance you're after, captivating the person of your dreams becomes easy as pie.

Regarding finances, you can use persuasion to sell more products or services, ace any interview, get your boss to give you a raise, motivate employees, and thrive in your career.

Persuasion improves your health indirectly. How? If you can handle issues regarding relationships and money, then you incur a lot less stress than most people. And you probably already know that stress is the main cause of many diseases. So by knowing how to persuade people effectively, your stress significantly decreases and you'll have a healthier disposition in life.

The key factor that makes persuasion so effective is that you rely on appeal rather than force, which makes people decide for themselves that they want to be in a situation in which you can change their views and actions. People like the idea that they independently make decisions on their own and for their own good, and persuasion does that very effectively.

This book aims to provide you with the necessary tools and training to win in the game of life. I'll teach you how to attain the ideal persuasion mindset and power up your belief that you can persuade anyone. I'll guide you step by step on how to prepare efficiently, overcome the challenges that you might encounter, and make the most out of your persuasion efforts. Then we'll dive into the persuasion secrets that will give you the upper hand in relationships and sales. You'll discover how to make people like you (even to the point of giving up their lives for you), skillfully handle (and give) criticisms and advice, conquer people who make your life miserable, and sell like crazy! You'll also learn about unusually powerful ways to apply the laws of persuasion, as well as body language secrets to be the best persuader you can be!

This book is direct to the point and easy to read, as I clearly explain the information in simple details. I also give plenty of stories and examples you can relate to, so you can fully understand and grasp the ideas.

So if you're excited and ready to transform your life, turn to the next page now and let's get started!

1

The Forgotten First 5 Steps to Selling Anyone Anything

Before persuading others, you must **believe** beyond any shadow of a doubt that your persuasion efforts will succeed, that you are capable of successfully persuading your target person. Your thoughts must be focused on your objective.

Never show any negative or self-defeating emotions. You don't want to go out there having thoughts like: "I'm not sure if I can ever persuade him" or "What if I won't be able to do it?"

Many people can see right through you. They can sense your fear and anxiety. Be absolutely calm and relaxed.

You must constantly think of the positive outcome of the persuasion scenario, and enjoy that experience beforehand. You must actually feel what you would be feeling upon effectively persuading him. In all cases, your intention must always be focused towards achieving a win-win outcome.

Believing in yourself first is vital. After all, you can't expect people to buy your idea if you yourself are not convinced. The way you present yourself, your tone of voice, and the amount of conviction in your words all give away how much you trust your own idea.

If you want to persuade other people to see things your way, you'd better stand up straighter, sound more confident, and smile more often (unless the topic doesn't call for it). And the most important thing is to believe in your ability to persuade and the positive outcome of your actions.

If you're selling something, you must **believe** in your product and be proud to offer it to others. If you're not assured in the ability of your product to satisfy or fulfill your customers' needs, then it would be very difficult to persuade them of your proposal. You would also suffer from internal conflict because your words or actions are inconsistent with your inner belief.

What you believe in can have a dramatic impact on your life, even if it's not real. Have you heard the news about the man who froze to death inside a refrigerated box car? He believed there was no escape and he was going to freeze to death. And he indeed froze to death. But after they discovered him a day later, they found that the refrigeration system was broken! And because heat couldn't escape from the inside of the car, it was actually warmer in the box car than the outside!

The unlucky man used the power of belief to his disadvantage. But now that you're aware, you can benefit from that same power to help you become a better persuader and achieve almost anything you set your mind to.

So how can you develop your belief to help you persuade more effectively? Here are some belief boosters that have been proven to work...

Belief Booster # 1:
Use the "As If" Technique

Act as if you are the person you want to be. Act as if you are already in possession of whatever you long to have. Think, act, and feel like a true master persuader. Be obsessed with your goal. If you think you are easily manipulated and non-persuasive, then that is what you will become unless you properly change your mindset.

Researchers have long claimed that our subconscious mind cannot differentiate a real event over one that is vividly imagined. So use this to your advantage. If you want to become the best persuader you can be, then imagine yourself influencing, convincing, and motivating people in different situations.

If you're going to speak in public, imagine yourself giving a motivational speech to a big audience. Fill in as much sensory details as possible. How many men and how many women are listening to you? What background music are you hearing? What do the flowers around you smell like? Are the lights just right? How loud is the audience clapping after you've given your speech?

The more vivid your thoughts, the more you increase your chances of actually believing in them happening.

Belief Booster # 2:
Dig Past Accomplishments

Ask yourself, "What compliment did I receive from people before that made me believe in my abilities? What have I achieved that made me feel proud of myself?"

Go down memory lane and remember the times you have successfully persuaded, convinced, or motivated someone. Here are some things to consider:

1) What did you do to convince your crush to be your girlfriend (or boyfriend)?
2) What did you do to persuade your boss to agree to your request?

3) What did you do to motivate someone to perform better?
4) How did you negotiate with your parents to get a larger allowance?

You may not be aware of it, but there are countless times that you have successfully persuaded people. Write down those instances, and think of how you may apply them in your current situation or future use.

When you think about your past accomplishments and feel good about them, you will increase your belief in yourself. After all, if you have done it before, you can do it again!

But what if you can't remember or find any relevant past experience or achievements? Then do # 3 below...

Belief Booster # 3:
Do It Once

A very effective way to boost your belief in something is to simply do it, even if it's just once.

For a long time, I'd been afraid of talking in front of my class. I thought that my voice sounded bad and that my actions were awkward. But once a teacher asked me to recite a poem in front of the class, I was able to deliver. And from that day on, I knew that I could do it again.

But what if you're having doubts on actually doing it? Let's say you're afraid to invite your crush for a date because you're not convinced she will accept your invitation. In this case, you can "practice" by inviting another person (perhaps a friend or someone whom you're more comfortable with) to a friendly dinner. When she accepts, you'd have formed a belief that you can do it. Invite another person and as the experiences pile up, your belief builds up as well.

Belief Booster # 4:
Read about People Who Have Done It

You've probably heard the famous story about Roger Bannister. He was the first person who ran a mile in less than 4 minutes. For many years, people believed it was impossible to run a mile within 4 minutes. But after Roger successfully did it, many other individuals were able to do it as well. Why? Because they finally believed that it can be done!

Read about people who have already succeeded in what you want to do. Find out how they think, what their habits are, and what actions they took to achieve their goals. If you're afraid of talking to others, read about famous motivational speakers and learn how they speak and connect with people. If you want to develop your belief that you can sell many products, read about successful salespeople who have "been there and done that."

Once you know that others have done it, you will increase your belief that you can do it, too!

Belief Booster # 5:
Anchor It

Imagine the power if you could just do a simple act, and you'll instantly be able to change your mood or amplify your belief.

When I mention the word oranges, your mind processes

the image, your mouth may begin to water, and you may even remember the times when you and your special someone were enjoying and eating the oranges together.

Here's another example.

Have you watched a movie that was so touching it made you cry? In one of the movie's most moving scenes, there was sad background music. Two months later, you're listening to the radio. You hear the same sad song from that movie. You suddenly remember the scene, the actors, the emotions, and even the person seated next to you who was also crying two months ago. You feel the sensation all over again. You recollect the sentimental mood because of that same music. The music has become an anchor for you.

What is an anchor? An anchor is a compelling and influential connection of something seen, heard, touched, smelled, or tasted with a specific memory or representation. You associate something experienced in the past with a state correlating to the present.

The key to successful anchoring is to stimulate the appropriate emotion in its most intense state. There are 5 steps involved:

Step 1: Reflect on a time when you were successfully influencing or motivating someone. If you don't have any relevant past experiences, just imagine that you're doing it (watching related videos or reading success stories can help elicit your desired image and emotion.). Engage yourself thoroughly in that wonderful feeling. See, hear, taste, smell, and feel everything around you.

Step 2: Once you're in the peak state of your thoughts

and feelings, create an anchor. You may clench your fist in excitement, say "Awesome!" out loud, squeeze your thumb and middle finger together, or just do anything distinct you can think of - as long as it's something that creates intensity within you when it brings you back to that moment.

Step 3: Let go of the anchor and break out of that state.

Step 4: Repeat Steps 1 to 3 many times. Get into your peak mental and emotional state, anchor it, and then let it go. Do this again and again to strengthen your anchor. The more intense and vivid the experience, the better an anchor you will create.

Step 5: Test your anchor. If it didn't build up your belief or whatever feelings you'd like to create, evaluate. Some possible reasons why it's not working could be:

- Your state may not be strong or intense enough. The more senses involved (sight, hearing, smell, taste, feeling), the better.
- Your timing might be off. You might not have anchored at the peak experience.
- Your anchor might not be unique. Using a smile as an anchor won't work effectively because you do it all the time (but it might work if you use a smile that is unusually different).
- You might not have repeated the anchor exactly as you did it. If thumping the right side of your chest is your anchor, then thumping the left side of your chest or applying a different pressure won't work.

After careful evaluation, you should be able to determine the real cause of the issue. Repeat steps 1 to 5 again, this time making the needed adjustment to make the anchor work.

Tip: *B*oost the power of your anchors by stacking. You could stack up your states (experiences), your stimuli (anchors), or both.

To stack up your states, recall a time when you have successfully persuaded someone in the past. Then install your anchor. After going through the 5 steps above, recall another time when someone agreed to your proposal. Then do the 5 steps above again. Repeat the process (with each experience different from the others, but with the same goal).

To stack up your stimuli, you could install more than one anchor simultaneously for each state. For example, instead of just beating your chest or saying "Roar!" at your peak state, you could do both of them at the same time.

Do both stacking and you would have intensified the power of your anchor.

Summary Outline

I.   Before persuading others, you must believe beyond any shadow of a doubt that your persuasion efforts will succeed.

II.   Five Ways To Boost Your Belief:

      A. Use the "As If" Technique.
      B. Dig Past Accomplishments.
      C. Do It Once.
      D. Read About People Who Have Done It.
      E. Anchor It.

2

The 5 Steps to Creating an Unstoppable Battle Plan

"Success depends upon previous preparation, and without such preparation there is sure to be failure."
~o~Confucius~o~

Preparing your persuasion battle plan is more important than the actual persuading itself. Here are 5 simple steps to prepare you for successful persuasion...

Step # 1:
<u>Determine Your "What" and "Why."</u>

The first thing you need to do is to know exactly the results you want to create. You can never truly accomplish something if you're not clear about the outcome. But when you know exactly what you want to do or happen, everything around you conspires to bring you to the path that you desire to accomplish.

If you want to get a salary raise, know exactly how much of an increase you'd like. If you want to sell more products, determine the minimum quantities you want to sell and at what price. If you want your kids to behave, identify the exact rules and responsibilities you want them to follow. The more specific and clear your desired end result, the better your chances of persuading.

Another important thing is to have a big enough "why." Know "why" you want the other person to agree with you. Why do you want to accomplish this?

If you want your spouse to agree with you to spending less on non-essential needs, find out why you want to do that. You could say that it would help the kids go through college or accumulate enough funds to start a small business. When your "why" is strong enough, your will to succeed intensifies!

Step # 2:
Study the Person You're Going to Persuade.

Know as much info as you can about him. Know his way of thinking, his behavior, his beliefs and opinions, his values, his dreams and ambitions, his failures, his strengths and weaknesses, etc.

You have to enter his inner world. Find out how he thinks, feels, and acts. Explore his wishes, hopes, fantasies, or fears. Ask, "What would I (feel, do, think, etc.) if I were him?" The more you know about him, the more you'll be able to come up with persuasion tactics to fit his needs or counter his objections.

If you want to get a rich old man to donate money to a certain charity, you won't get him to part with his cash just by asking him to (unless he really is the charitable type). However, if you knew what his weaknesses are (for the sake of proving a point, let's say he has a weakness for beautiful women), you can use it to persuade him to make a donation. Ask one of your prettiest volunteers to do the solicitation, or casually remark that women go crazy over charitable and distinguished tycoons.

Tip: Males and females think and act differently. Most males are more dominant in their left brain, while most females are more dominant in their right brain. Most males stay silent when others are telling them something, while most females say things like "right" "uh – huh" or "yup" to imply that they are listening.

One effective way to know more about a certain person is to search for him on Facebook. Almost anyone already has a Facebook account. And if he's like millions of people who are connecting on Facebook, he'll be posting his thoughts and experiences, as well as pictures. From there, you can figure out his habits, likes/dislikes, behavior, and other important facts about him. You'll then be able to come up with better ways of persuading him from his point of perspective and customize your plans to fit his model of the world.

In due time, you'll be able to determine what he naturally moves closer to or farther away from. Believe me, this will help save you a lot of time. It's always easier to avoid a mistake than to have to clean the mess up afterwards.

Step # 3:
<u>Devise Your Strategy.</u>

Determine your desired end result, then work your way backwards to devise a good strategy in persuading him. Predict the possible problems or challenges that may occur, and list down the steps on how you will be able to deal with each.

In this step, you will also go through the laws of persuasion and other techniques discussed in the succeeding chapters, so you can pick the right ones to apply in your own situation. I've included lots of case scenarios and examples, so you'll know what to apply when you encounter a similar situation.

Because we are not living in a perfect world, not all

techniques produce the same powerful results (it all depends on many factors including the timing, the person's state of mind, the way you apply them, etc.). In this case, there's no harm utilizing another method and learning from the experience.

Step # 4:
Use Visualizations and Affirmations.

After you have devised your strategy, play the scenes in your mind like a movie. This is important because you get to actually practice and feel the entire persuasion process. Focus on your mission or goal. You have to visualize the entire persuasion process you will be doing. Imagine yourself persuading your target person; indulge in the satisfying feeling of having your desired outcome achieved in visually perfect detail.

Engage in self-talk with intensity, passion, and enthusiasm. When you persuade others, do it with feelings. Affirmations are supposed to be stated in the present tense, but your mind will say, "That's not true" if your affirmations are far from reality or if you have some tinge of doubt. So say your statements in the present progressive form.

For example, if you're still learning to become a master salesman, instead of saying "I am a master salesman," say "I am becoming a master salesman." As you become more skilled and gain more experience, your confidence increases proportionately, until you can say your affirmations in the present tense: "I am a master salesman."

Want to borrow your friend John's car? Say to yourself, "I am successfully persuading John to lend me his car." Say it out loud! Say it 10 times, 20 times, 30 times, until you feel the fire and confidence within you exploding like firecrackers on

New Year's Eve.

Now remember to say it in the present progressive tense. Say "I AM successfully persuading John to lend me his car," and not "I WILL successfully persuade John to lend me his car." You've got to have it now, not in the future! So be relentless and assertive. Then picture yourself saying it to him with utmost assurance. Visualize John smiling and obeying your every will. Envision him as a little boy giving you the keys to his beautiful car. He can't help but follow your every command.

These principles apply even if the person you're going to persuade is far away. Let's say you're a salesperson who's going to write your client an email regarding your product. Say aloud, "I AM expertly persuading {name of client} to buy my product. He's buying my product because it's the best he's ever seen. He's happy using my product." Say it many times with firmness and assurance. Then envision him buying and enjoying your product. Imagine him thanking you over and over because he has gotten more than his money's worth. Visualize him treating you as a very good friend because you gave him the very best deal he could ever lay his hands on. Then write your email. Pour all your emotions into that letter. Not ordinary emotions, but genuinely pure and caring emotions that come from the heart. Feel your love for this client. Write things that would make him happy and willing to do business with you. Even if he's far away from you, he will feel the aura of your presence with your email.

Step # 5:
Choose The Right Mood And Time.

At this point, you're almost ready to do the actual act of persuading and you're excited! But hold on! You need to check first if he's in the right mood and if the timing is appropriate.

Become more observant first. Don't jump in front of your target and confront him head on. It's all about subtlety and getting a "feel" for the other person. Determine if the person you're persuading is in a good mood or not. Know if he's busy or swamped with tasks to do. He will be more responsive to your request if he's in a good frame of mind.

When he's not in the mood or when he's time-pressed, your persuasion efforts may just fall into deaf ears because he will not give you attention. In some cases, a person can easily agree to your requests when he's busy and distracted. But this will only backfire because he will feel tricked that he gave in to you at a "vulnerable" time. So never do this.

Now even if you think he's in a good mood, ask first if you can have a few minutes of his time. If he says it's not a good time, ask for a time that fits his schedule. Be flexible and patient and your efforts will reap the rewards.

Summary Outline

I. Preparing your persuasion battle plan is more important than the actual persuading itself.

II. Five Simple Steps to Prepare You for Successful Persuasion:

 A. Determine Your "What" and "Why."
 B. Study the Person You're Going to Persuade.
 C. Devise Your Strategy.
 D. Use Visualizations and Affirmations.
 E. Choose the Right Mood and Time.

3

The Most Common Persuasion Challenges
And How to Overcome Them

Persuading someone isn't always a fun walk in the park. Challenges are bound to show themselves, so you've got to be ready when they show up.

Challenge # 1:
Overcoming Restrictions

Keep in mind that not all people can be persuaded. If that person has any restriction, then you may never be able to persuade him, and that would be a waste of your valuable time.

Remember that the aim of persuading others is to achieve a win-win situation. Always propose something that will be beneficial to both of you.

Let's say your prospect is a financial genius, and he never intends to incur any interest expense. He always pays his credit card on time. Now it will be fruitless if you talk for minutes to convince him to join your "credit card balance transfer" program.

How about if a lady whose religion prohibits her to eat pork? No matter how delectable or appetizing your dish is, if it contains pork, she will never eat it no matter what you do.

In every persuasion attempt, remember that the person you're persuading must not have any restrictions; or else, you'll just be wasting both your prospect's time and yours. You might also be perceived as disrespectful. But there are still ways to deal with such restrictions. One way is to appeal to a higher value.

Let's say your friend Kate has a firm belief that it's unethical to invade someone's privacy. But if she suspects her son of taking drugs, then you can persuade her to go through her son's cabinet and personal belongings to confirm her suspicion. In this case, the higher value (her love and concern for her son) overcomes her other value (respect for someone's privacy).

Challenge # 2:
Getting Attention

To persuade effectively, you must get people's attention. However, too many things are often craving for our attention. Because of this, we have developed a sort of filter to shield out those we deem not important.

The question is: How do we get past the human filter, in order for our message to be heard and for others to pay attention to us?

People pay attention only to those messages they like to hear, so give it to them. Step into their shoes, adjust your message to be in line with what they like to hear, and tell them.

They also need to be motivated in order to give attention to you. If they are not motivated, their attention span is short. If their present state is not conducive to paying attention (for example, they are depressed or lonely), they are less likely to listen to you. So they have to be in the right mood when you impart your message.

As I've said before, it's important to be sensitive to people's present mood and state of mind. There is always a right time to communicate with people, and doing it when they're not in a good mood can significantly reduce your chances to persuade well. When you've found they're in a "persuadable" state, you can augment their positive frame of mind by developing rapport, and using the right body language and verbal methods (you'll learn them all in later chapters).

And of course, people are more likely to listen to you and remember what you have to say if they trust, respect, or like you. Emotions play a big part. If you made people feel good in any way, they will tend to listen to you and remember you.

Interest plays a big part as well. If people are not interested, your message will not pass through their filters no matter how hard you try to impress your message in their minds. Do you notice how you can learn something so much faster because you're passionate about the subject, but can't get anything in your mind if you hate the topic?

<u>Here are some fantastic tips to grab and maintain people's attention:</u>

✓ **Create a controversial or eye-opening statement.**
   • This must literally stop whatever is consuming their mind as of the moment.

Example: *"Nita has already won 3 bingo games in the past week, and she says there is a secret technique to winning!"*

✓ **Ask an engaging question.**
   • Don't ask something answerable by "Yes" or "No." Ask a question that will stop their train of thought, a question that will distract them from what they're thinking presently and allow them to focus on the question.

Examples:

- *"If you could go to any place on earth, where is your ideal vacation spot?"*
- *"Can you remember the time when you felt so proud of your accomplishment?"*

These questions allow them to "escape" their present state of thought and picture instances in their mind.

✓ **Arouse their curiosity.**

- Master persuaders successfully entice people to come running to them because they know how to arouse curiosity. Once in a state of curiosity, people will have a dying itch to satisfy it.

Examples of curiosity-arousing statements:

- *To someone who is broke, these words would strike a chord:* "Research has found that the richest people on earth all know the same secrets that the rest of the world never knew. I finally discovered what they are."
- *To a basketball player, this would be very interesting:* "I have read a book on how to increase your vertical jump by at least 5 inches."

I'm sure the target people you're persuading will never stop until they know what you know.

Challenge # 3:
Being Believed In.

Chapter One shows you how to believe in yourself. This challenge is about other people believing in you and your message. People go through a 2-step belief process. First, they measure the "believability" of a person, and then they gauge the "believability" of the message of that person.

Here are some guidelines to become more believable.

1) **Believe in yourself and your message first, before attempting to make anyone believe in you.** Your own conviction will manifest in your words and actions. You've probably heard about cult leaders who relayed their messages with such intensity and unfettered emotions that the audience would do anything being told to them, even if it means ending their own lives! But of course, you should use this only for good means.

2) **Be consistent.** Establish trust so people are more likely to believe you. Then say words that are honest and consistent with your actions and body language, so your future messages are more credible. Make sure that your voice volume, pitch, and tone, as well as your gestures, are appropriate for the current situation. Just imagine the insult and awkwardness if you're attending a funeral and you suddenly laugh. Be aware of your words and movement always.

3) **Be yourself.** Don't be someone you're not. If you're in love with someone, for example, but have qualities not compatible with him and fake your behavior or "wing" things just to impress him, sooner or later, you'll be found out. Don't claim to be someone you're not.

4) **Never lie.** One lie, just one lie you say, will make people doubt whether all the past things you've said are true. That will ruin their trust in you, and they might never believe you again.

Whatever you say from then on, they will scrutinize first and ask themselves, "Can that be true?" And when you're persuading people, you can't possibly allow them to have any doubts in their minds!

Summary Outline

I. Challenges are bound to show themselves when you're persuading people, so you've got to be ready when they show up.

II. Persuasion Challenges include:

    A. Overcoming Restrictions.
       Solution: Appeal to a higher value.

    B. Getting Attention.
       Solutions:

       o *Create a controversial or eye-opening statement.*
       o *Ask an engaging question.*
       o *Arouse their curiosity.*

    C. Being Believed In.
       Solutions:

       o Believe in yourself and your message first, before attempting to make anyone believe in you.
       o Be consistent.
       o Be yourself.
       o Never lie.

4

Eight Factors for Maximum Persuasion Success!

There are eight key factors that could dramatically increase your chances of persuasion success. Before you go out persuading, read and study these keys over and over. Ignoring any one of them could slash down your success rate significantly.

Key # 1:
Be Crystal Clear in Imparting Your Message

When you say, "He's mad," do you mean he's angry or do you mean he's crazy? Whenever you're going to say or write something that is vague or may lead to miscommunication, it's highly recommended that you change the words in a way that imparts a clear message.

Key # 2:
Watch Out for Body Language Signs.

You might not know if the other party is getting bored or anxious unless you're keen on observing his gestures or movements. You can always "stop the bleeding" and adjust to the situation early before it gets any worse. (Chapter 16 talks about reading and using body language.)

Watch out for the body signals that you are giving away as well. You might be pouting your lips, breathing heavily, shaking your head, or rolling your eyes without you being aware that you're offending others.

Watch your language too. If saying "Whatever," "Oh

brother," or "Yeah right" is part of your lingo, practice taking them out of your vocabulary.

Key # 3:
Start Your Discussion on the Right Track.

One of the biggest mistakes people make in persuasion is that they start talking about a topic or situation that the other person is not yet aware of or familiar with.

I have a friend who often dives into the middle of a story or subject, which leaves me (and I assume many other people) clueless on what he's talking about. It's important to start your discussion on a point that people can relate to, preferably from the very beginning, unless you're sure that they already know the foundation of the topic of discussion.

Key # 4:
Give Them a Summary or an Overall Glimpse of The Big Picture.

This is vital when talking about something that takes a little (or a lot more) time to comprehend. This way, they can better relate the discussion to the big picture and "absorb" what you're saying.

Key # 5:
Never Assume nor Disrespect.

To think that others have the same likes, attitudes, or behavior as we do is often the reason why many persuasion efforts fail. Everyone is unique, so you cannot say that because you like something, others will like it too. Everyone is extraordinary, so we have to respect each other's uniqueness.

Each person has his own beliefs. You must never disrespect or disagree with another person's beliefs even if it is contrary to your own. You must model his belief as much as possible, or at least appear to have the same belief as him.

When you don't oppose his beliefs, opinions or values, he tends to feel comfortable with you and trust you. You must let him know that you value his words, and respect what he has to say.

Even if you don't like his idea, at least appear to consider his opinion. This shows respect and humility. Say something like, "You've got a good point there. I'll certainly take that into consideration."

If you simply can't agree with his beliefs, just keep your opinions to yourself; opposing his views will not result to any good. Instead, you may ask him to talk more about his views or experiences. By doing this, you're letting him know that you're listening and empathizing, and these two acts will earn you his respect.

If you hold a position in the government and another person believes that all politicians are "corrupt" or "dishonest," you may say something like, "Seems like you had an unfortunate experience. Can you tell me more?"

More importantly, never force him to accept what you're saying. The more you force him and restrict his options, the more he'll reject your proposal. What you must do is persuade him in a natural, smooth-flowing manner where he'll feel like accepting your idea is all part of the process.

Key # 6:

Pay Attention to What Is Being Said Instead of Thinking What You'll Say Next.

This may be a little difficult for you to do initially, as you're thinking of the best way to respond to him in the most influential way possible.

That's why it's critical to practice and enhance your persuasion skills until it becomes a part of you. Listen attentively and don't interrupt while he's talking. Wait a second or two before you speak. Avoid changing subjects because this indicates your disinterest.

Key # 7:
Make Sure You Completely Understand His Message.

You can say something like, "So what you're saying is (your understanding of their message)." He will correct you in case you misinterpreted.

Key # 8:
Practice, Track Your Progress, and Learn From Every Experience.

This key involves 4 sub-steps:

A. Practice, practice, practice ...

Don't just read, but apply what you've learned. Master the persuasion techniques in this book in such a way that you will apply them without conscious effort, so you can focus on the other person without needing to think of what to do next.

B. Observe people's reaction or response when you apply your persuasion techniques on them.

Learn from your experiences, then plan your future courses of action and improve on your methods. Some people even videotape their persuasion escapades, so they can watch the video over and over to see how people responded or reacted, where they went wrong, and how they can improve.

C. Ask for feedback.

Ask feedback from your closest relatives or friends regarding the way you communicate. Sometimes, we are blind to our own flaws. Have you ever gotten angry with someone for doing an act that you sometimes do to others also? Why wouldn't you get mad at yourself, but you get upset when other people do the same thing to you? That's because our ego sometimes makes it hard for us to detect our own faults.

So if you want to know if you are communicating at a level that is respectable, likeable, or influential, don't just rely on your own opinion about yourself. Ask your closest contacts regarding their observations of you when you are talking with them or with other people.

There are other things you can ask feedback for, like the way you motivate or persuade others, the consistency of your body language with your words, etc.

D. Record your persuasion attempts.

Write down or record the persuasion method that you have done, the errors you have observed which you can improve on, and the revised action that you would do to achieve better results.

Keep on improving until you've found the best ways to

persuade. Take note, however, that each person has his own unique qualities; so you may also want to note down the person to which you've applied a particular method so you can apply a unique tactic for that specific individual.

Summary Outline

I. There are eight key factors that could dramatically increase your chances of persuasion success.

II. Eight Key Factors:

    A. Be Crystal Clear in Imparting Your Message.

    B. Watch Out for Body Language Signs.

    C. Start Your Discussion on the Right Track.

    D. Give Them a Summary or an Overall Glimpse of The Big Picture.

    E. Never Assume nor Disrespect.

    F. Pay Attention to What Is Being Said Instead of Thinking What You'll Say Next.

    G. Make Sure You Completely Understand His Message.

    H. Practice, Track Your Progress, and Learn From Every Experience.

       o Practice, practice, practice …

       o Observe people's reaction or response when you apply your persuasion techniques on them.

       o Ask for feedback.

       o Record your persuasion attempts.

5

Ten Steps to Make Anyone Like You... A LOT!

Being liked by people is often more important than having authority or talent. There are some individuals who don't have much skill or intelligence, but they are successful because people love them and would do anything for them.

Doctors spend more time with patients they like; they ask them to come back more often for further check-ups. Judges or juries give lesser penalties to guilty parties whom they like. Students learn faster if they like their teachers.

Joe Girard, the "World's Greatest Salesman" as listed in the Guinness Book of World Records, uses the principle of likeability a lot. In his career, he has sold 13,001 cars and has held unbelievable sales records. His secret? Every month, he would send a holiday greeting card to all of his customers totaling 13,001. The card would only say, "I like you" with his name on it. His customers liked him back, a lot!

So how would you go about convincing other people to like you? Being liked is not a forced action. This chapter explains some astonishing ways to make people like you very much!

Technique # 1:
Make as Many Friends as You Can.

The more friends you have, the better your chances of having more people like you. Having many friends means that you have a support group and safety net who you can rely on - and ask help from - any time you need one.

If you're a professional and want to increase your clients, ask your friends for referrals. They will be more than glad to help you out. That's because your friends like and trust you.

To increase your friends, expose yourself as much as you can. Join social events, parties, organizations, etc. The more people you meet, the more chances you have of making the right connections. You can also use social media sites like Facebook to your advantage.

Find your friends' contacts and invite them to add you (since you already have mutual friends, they are more likely to accept your invitation). Then you can nurture and develop your relationships with them. The best way is to meet them face-to-face. If this is not possible, at least call them on the phone. Email is your last option, because you sense less emotion through email.

Speaking of exposure, the more someone sees you or communicates with you, the more he will grow to like you. So get out there, and make yourself seen and heard more often!

Technique # 2:
Give Sincere Compliments.

The best way to start a conversation and make a connection is to give a sincere and honest compliment. Pick out anything that strikes you about that person.

People love to hear something nice about themselves. So find something praise-worthy about them. It doesn't have to be too profound. It could be something as simple as "Hey, that's a cool watch" or "Oh my God, is that the newest Birkin?"

People feel good about hearing compliments, so try to express your delight more freely. However, don't overdo it and never give a forced or insincere compliment. Don't say you like something about a person when you don't mean it.

If you're not sure if your compliment is going to be regarded in the positive light, you can tell a third party (whom both of you know) what you like about - or how much you like - the person. Once your compliment reaches the recipient, your likeability rate increases a thousand fold in his eyes because it comes across as more genuine and sincere.

Technique # 3:
Focus On Them and Their Interests.

Since feeding their ego and being interested in them is one key to being liked, you can ask them what they do, what their hobbies are, or what they do for a living. You may also ask them personal things about their family, lifestyle, or their goals or dreams in life. Avoid talking about sensitive topics like politics and religion.

Become interested in what they have to say. If possible, ask them about things that reveal their values. Knowing their values is key to successful persuasion. After they're done sharing, they will tend to reciprocate and ask you the same questions. You'll then be able to share your own views, keeping in mind to not offend any of their principles or values.

However, let them do more of the talking and you, more of the listening. But don't just pretend to listen. Show genuine interest and make sincere comments.

If the other person decides to share some personal matters with you, it's important to empathize with him. If he has lost a person he loves, don't say, "Don't feel too bad. I've got worse things happening to my life right now." Just say, "You must be feeling bad now. If there's anything I can do to help, please call me immediately." Remember to put your own emotions aside so you can understand how he is feeling.

Now if he's talking about how ecstatic he is for winning the championship, don't tell your own story in winning your MVP award. This is his shining moment, so don't steal the spotlight. When you make him feel good, he will feel good when he's with you.

Technique # 4:
Smile Genuinely.

Without a good smile, you'll have a tough time getting people to warm up to you. I suggest practicing different smiles in front of the mirror to see which one looks best on you.

As you smile, think about different situations. You might want to think about the time your child first learned how to walk and see how your smile looks. Or you could think about how you won a contest and see how confident your smile looks in the mirror. The best smile is the kind of smile that makes people feel like they're special.

However, the smile must be genuine and sincere. Fake smiles are easily recognizable. To give a genuine smile, smile with your eyes. Think of happy moments and focus on his positive qualities. Avoid the habit of finding fault in others. Soon, you'll find that the person has some positive traits that you can truly feel good and smile about.

Technique # 5:

Say These 3 Magic Words More Often.

The three magic words are his name, "please" and "thank you."

Nothing could be more pleasing to someone's ears than hearing his own name being spoken. It gives him a sense of individuality. To remember a name easily the first time you hear it, associate the name with something familiar and say the name a few times to commit it to memory.

If his name is Douglas, you can visualize him walking his dog that is wearing eyeglasses (dog + glass = Douglas), then say his name a couple of times to remember it even better.

If one's name is the sweetest word to hear, "please" and "thank you" are tied at 2nd. However, don't just say a simple "thank you." Let the person know what you're thankful for.

Examples:
- *"George, thank you for helping me with my assignment."*
- *"Tina, would you please give this to our boss? Thank you for always being efficient."*

Technique # 6:
Offer Value.

Once you know his likes or passions, offer to do or give something related to it. Write down a list of your strengths or abilities, then refer to the list and see which one might complement his passions.

Example:
You found out that Ray loves to eat out. If one of your

skills is cooking, you could invite him to try out your recipe. If you don't know how to cook but know a friend who can, you may ask a favor from him to cook something very special for Ray. Or you could simply invite Ray to a fine dining restaurant and spend more time with him.

Sometimes though, you got to do a little digging to find out his interests, passions, and even problems. Ask questions such as:

"What do you want most out of life?"
"What types of situations do you treat as problems?"
"What do you wish to accomplish in the next few months?"
"Is there anything I can do to help you get what you want?"

Make sure you're not offending anyone. Since you don't know if a certain subject would offend the other party, it helps to ask questions like:

"What do you think about...?"
"What's your opinion on...?"
"How do you find the...?"

Also, watch out for key words that reveal his likes and dislikes. These words include *want, wish, like, need, help, hope, hate, dislike, problem, confused,* etc.

If he says, "I need to manage my time better," you could search for a video on YouTube or a free e-book that will help him to manage his time effectively.

Technique # 7:
Share Your Secrets.

People tend to trust you if you make them perceive that you're sharing a secret with them, especially one that is not normally shared. When you tell a secret, they tend to open up in response and drop their defenses. Say something like, "I'd like to share a secret with you, but please don't tell anyone" or "I should keep this to myself, but I'm going to tell you anyway because you're a good friend."

Technique # 8:
Make Him Laugh.

Laughter releases endorphins from our system. Endorphins are pain killers that can give us a sense of happiness or exhilaration. When you make someone laugh, you automatically make him feel more at ease and comfortable with you. He will get to like you and be more open in his communication with you.

Buy a few joke books and find the funniest jokes you can tell. Go through some videos on YouTube and if you find anything that makes you laugh a ton, share it. He will associate the humor in the video, and happiness he felt, with you.

Part of having a sense of humor is being able to laugh at your flaws. If you did something embarrassing, don't act as if nothing happened. Some people think that ignoring the embarrassing situation could save their ego from getting hurt, but it's actually the other way around. Laughing it off shows your humility and confidence to handle such circumstances in a likeable manner.

Technique # 9:
Find Similarities.

We all want to be around people who have the same behaviors, experiences, beliefs, and values as ours. We feel more at ease with those who have similar backgrounds as ours... whether it's religion, culture, or race. Similarities may also range from routines to hobbies to personality - anything you can find to link yourself to them. And if you have identical physical (especially facial) features, that's a plus too.

So if you really want someone to like you, you have to find any commonalities between you and the person you're persuading - and let him be aware of these similarities - in order to create a comfortable environment between the both of you and establish a bond. By finding a common ground, you make him feel that you understand his point of view or share his opinions.

Technique # 10:
Mirror Him.

Mirroring is one of the most popular persuasion techniques for building rapport and getting someone to like you because it makes him feel that both of you are on the "same level." It involves you trying to copy whatever the other person is doing while communicating with him, in order to establish some sort of bond. This is commonly observed in people exhibiting similar postures, gestures, or voice tonality.

However, mirroring is easily goofed up by many people. How? Well, mirroring should be natural, not forced; but many people are too blatant with their actions. Mirroring should not be confused with mimicry. You should act with courtesy and caution. Never let the person you're mirroring be aware of what you're doing. The effect of mirroring works even if he is not consciously aware that you're doing it, because you're influencing his subconscious mind.

There are various aspects you can mirror in order to establish rapport. Some examples include:

- Breathing rate - Is it slow, fast, or moderate?
- Posture - Is he standing straight, leaning forward, or slouching?
- Movements/gestures - Does he use his hands to express himself better? Is he crossing his legs? Are his legs bouncing?
- Voice quality – Is it loud or soft? High pitch or low pitch?
- Speed of rate in speaking - Does he speak fast or slowly?
- Types of words used – Repeat the exact words he said. Say, "Let me see if I got it right. So you want to... and you need to go to..." If he said he wants to go to the

party, don't say "So you want to go to the *celebration*." Even though "party" and "celebration" are identical in meaning, mirroring and rapport-building works if you repeat the exact words he said.

You may also do some crossover mirroring. For example, you talk at the same rate as his breathing. Or you scratch your chin every time his eyes blink.

After some time, touch your nose, cross your legs, or make any movement. If the prospect follows your action or movement, you have successfully mirrored him and he will subconsciously feel at ease with you. If not, then continue to mirror him.

You may also mirror the emotions or his state, BUT only if you're mirroring the positive. If the prospect is in an exciting and happy state, mirror his behavior or present condition. However, if he's depressed or anxious, or has some big emotional problems, never mirror him! Or you run the risk of actually absorbing his emotions.

Tip: Did you know that aside from mirroring, an actual physical mirror can be an effective persuasion tool? When you want to persuade someone, try to get him in front of a mirror. This allows him to be more "conscious" of himself, which makes him more receptive to your message.

Technique # 11:
Conform to His Primary Sense or Senses.

Although we have five senses – visual (sight), auditory (hearing), kinesthetic (touch or feeling), olfactory (smell), and gustatory (taste) - we tend to use a specific sense more than the others. The first three are the most commonly used, so we will focus on them.

Visual people tend to speak fast and take shallow breaths. They use words that pertain to sight such as *look, seem, view, perceive, imagine, etc.* For example, they say, "It *seems* like you're on a roll" or "The presentation *looks* good to me."

Auditory people tend to speak at a moderate pace and breathe deeply. They use words that pertain to hearing such as *listen, hear, sounds like, etc.* For example, they say, "It *sounds* like fun" or "I love to *hear* you say it."

Kinesthetic people tend to speak slowly and calmly, and take deep breaths. They use words that convey feeling or emotion such as *feel, contact, touch, etc.* For example, they say, "I *feel* the same way" or "I need to get in *touch* with you."

The key to using this technique is to talk and breathe the same way as him. Use similar words and do things that pertain to the primary sense he's using. You certainly don't like to speak fast to a kinesthetic person. Letting a visual person hear a motivational speech won't do much to inspire him either.

Once, I heard my little cousin say that her mother didn't love her. I found this odd, since I often hear her mother saying "I love you" to her, and she often takes my cousin out to go sightseeing or watch a movie. When I asked her why she would say something like that, my cousin said, "Mom's not hugging me, and she's not even kissing me before I go to sleep. I can't **feel** her love at all." So that's why! My cousin is a kinesthetic person but her mom was showing her love through the auditory and visual faculties. I quickly explained the process to her mom and she started to embrace, hug, and kiss my cousin often. Their relationship blossomed from then on.

Sometimes, more than one sense is involved - and they must be presented in the proper sequence - to make a person tick.

Let's say you noticed that your friend Jacob is depressed and you want to help him. Have him recall a time when he's totally happy and excited. Then ask him, "What made you feel great during that time? Was it something you saw or read? Was it something you heard? Or perhaps someone's touch made you feel that way?" If he answers that it was the time when his father said he loved and missed him so much, you now know his happiness "hot button" begins with auditory.

Next you ask, "After you heard him say that, what caused you to feel happy? Did you imagine something or hear anything else, or felt any other emotion?" If he says that he remembered the time when they were out in the woods stargazing, then his next hot button is of the visual type.

But his sequence may not be complete yet. You then ask him again, "After you heard him say that and you remembered your time together, what was the next thing that made you happy? Did you see something, or say something to yourself, or feel something else?" If he can add nothing else and feels totally happy at that moment, then his sequence is complete. His sequence is Auditory-Visual-Kinesthetic. He has heard something, recalled a past memory, and then felt happy.

Now you dig deeper and find out the inner aspects. You may ask, "What made you feel totally happy when you heard your father say that? Was it the words 'I love you?' Or was it the way he said it? Did he speak fast, slow, loudly, softly, or any other way? What did you recall? Was it radiant or massive? What colors did you see?"

After you have asked all this, you can talk to him in the same manner about how much people cared for him. Then tell him to visualize something identical with his past memory - with the same color, brightness and size as the image in his memory - and how happy he will feel afterward.

Summary Outline

I. Being liked by people is often more important than having authority or talent. There are some individuals who don't have much skill or intelligence, but they are successful because people love them and would do anything for them.

II. Eleven Ways To Make People Like You Very Much:

    A. Make as Many Friends as You Can.

    B. Give Sincere Compliments.

    C. Focus On Them and Their Interests.

    D. Smile Genuinely.

    E. Say These Three Magic Words More Often.

    F. Offer Value.

    G. Share Your Secrets.

    H. Make Him Laugh.

    I. Find Similarities.

    J. Mirror Him.

    K. Conform to His Primary Sense or Senses.

6

How to Give Criticisms & Advice That Actually Work

Have you ever encountered an experience when someone told you how fat (or thin) you've become? Maybe your boss has commented on how bad your work turned out to be. Or maybe you've heard from other folks how people view you as cold and unapproachable. Hurts, doesn't it?

Now let's turn the tables around. There are also times when you need to criticize people to help improve a certain aspect of their lives, but you don't like to hurt their feelings or ego.

So what can we do in these situations? Look no further. This chapter shows you how to handle and give criticism in the most positive light. You'll also learn how to get honest feedback from others (even if they don't intend to criticize), as well as dismiss any advice you won't be following without hurting their feelings.

How to Handle Criticisms without Losing Your Cool

You can never satisfy everyone in this world, which is why you have to know how to handle harsh words and offensive remarks. Here's how...

I. Clarify the details.

Because critics have the tendency to inflate the situation, ask them for quantifiable proof. But never ask in this way: "What makes you think that (what I did) was wrong?" Your question might be perceived as a defensive reaction to their criticism. There's a nicer and more subtle way to ask.

Before asking your question, it would help to say, "I don't understand" or "Let me get this straight" or "Please allow me to clarify." By saying any of these, you are not being defensive, but you're opening yourself for clarification.

Examples:
- *"**I don't understand**. What is it about my report that was offensive?"*
- *"**Please allow me to clarify**. In what way was the data inappropriate?"*
- *"**Let's get this straight**. What part of the presentation was inaccurate?"*

By asking this way, you will know the exact reason for their criticism, and you'll have a chance to give them the complete facts and evidences to support your case.

II. Reframe the criticism.

Instead of treating the criticism as a nasty insult, consider it as honest feedback to help you improve yourself.

When your boss tells you that your report still needs to be better, listen to everything he has to say. Which parts need to be redone? Which parts are already approved? Keep an open mind. You may have missed something important that your boss spotted right away, so it's actually a good thing that he told you about it. Ask your boss what you can do to make things better. It's a sign that you're willing to correct your mistakes and that you're committed to doing your job well.

By doing this, you'll be able to replace your anger or

frustration with gratitude. This puts you in the right frame of mind.

III. Use fogging.

When someone says that you're a slow learner, is that true or false? That may be true if you're compared to someone like Isaac Newton, but it may also be false if you're compared to the fictional character, Mr. Bean.

In a general sense, what he says may be partially true, so why fight it? Admit that what he said might be right in order to diffuse the criticism or attack. When he finds out you're not affected, it will discourage him. It's like saying "Who cares?" or "So what?" in a gentle fashion. Words most commonly used when fogging are:

"You're probably right."
"I agree."
"Sometimes I think that way too."
"You have a point."
"I can see why you would say that."
"That could be true."

Example:
Mr. Y: You look so ugly today. You didn't look like this a few weeks ago.
Mr. Z: I agree. My face has become ugly because all these sleepless nights are causing countless pimples to appear.
Mr. Y: In fact, you look like a pimple with a face on it.
Mr. Z: You're probably right. I could go to a dermatologist and have them do something about my ugly face.
Mr. Y: And your clothes. It looks like it's been worn by the victim in a massacre film.
Mr. Z: You have a point, you know. I may sometimes be so

thrifty I have to buy the lowest quality outfit.

Mr. Y: Thrifty is the understatement of the century. You're so cheap you can't even buy yourself some ramen noodles.

Mr. Z: I can see why you would say that. I may be very cheap at times.

Mr. Y: The worst part is, your breath is as terrible as your looks.

Mr. Z: Sometimes I think that way too. My breath may stink so bad it could render anyone unconscious.

Mr. Y: You act like a spineless coward, the way you're answering me.

Mr. Z: I agree. I may be acting like a spineless coward sometimes.

Through fogging, you accept the criticism in as far as whatever may be true in it (as stated by the critic). The critic will see it as a hopeless measure to argue with you any further. This is an effective way to handle criticism without being defensive.

IV. Apply negative assertion.

What if the criticism is absolutely true? Then you must willingly accept the criticism, but you don't have to take the guilt trip. Negative assertion allows you to be more tolerant of your own faults and eases any negative feelings the critic may have by admitting your mistakes, without having to resort to remorseful repentance. Here's how a son used negative assertion in his conversation with his father:

Dad: Son, I saw your report card and I am very much disappointed with your grades.

Son: You're right, Dad. I should do something to improve my grades.

Dad: Well, you should! I think you're spending so much time on extracurricular activities that you're sacrificing your studies. Why not focus on just your studies?

Son: These activities do take up so much of my time, don't they, Dad? I will manage my time and learn to prioritize. If needed, I'll forgo some of my extracurricular activities.

V. Reverse the roles.

Sometimes, people just blame you for circumstances beyond your control. If they're in your position, they won't be able to resolve the problem too, but they blame you anyway.

To make them understand what you're going through, ask something like, "If you're in my position, what would you do and how would you feel?" By doing this, they will at least realize how their words are affecting you.

VI. Counter the criticism.

It's important to use a proper rebuttal when you hear words of discouragement or disagreement. If your spouse says, "We shouldn't take this vacation yet because I have tons of work to do that is stressing me out," you could say something like, "That's why we should go. You need to relax and recharge in order to be more productive." Here are some other ways to counter their criticism or objection.

a. **It's Not That....** - When someone has an objection, you can always negate the objection and point out the benefits / advantages.

Example:
Critic: Your plan is too risky.
You: It's not that it's risky. This plan will be the cornerstone of our success.

b. Negative Outcome - You can successfully overcome criticism by pointing out the negative consequences of not doing the action.

Example:
<u>Critic:</u> *You're too untalented to join the contest.*
<u>You:</u> *If I join, I either win or lose. But I lose 100% if I don't join. And I wouldn't want to spend the rest of my life thinking "What if..."*

c. Positive Benefits - You can also point out the positive effects or benefits of changing their belief.

Example:
<u>Critic:</u> *It's too stressful to study Law.*
<u>You:</u> *How could studying Law give you the brighter future, rewarding career, and dream fulfillment you've always longed for?*

d. Opposing Instances - Think of occasions or instances when their criticism or belief has been proven wrong.

Example:
<u>Critic:</u> *I don't believe in God because I don't believe in things I can't see.*
<u>You:</u> *You can't see air, but you know it's there, right?*

e. Immunize against the criticism.

Here's a method to protect (or should I say "immunize") the people you know from criticisms that may hurt their feelings or ego. Let's say you have a child who is ready for his first day of school. He might come across some other students who might belittle or tease him. Before he meets other students, "immunize" him from any possible verbal attack by saying, "Son, you're going to meet other kids who might tell you that they are better or smarter than you. Just ignore them because what they are saying is wrong. Some kids are so insecure they'll discourage you from doing your best. But you know better now that I've told you this secret." By doing this, your child will be well prepared to face such an incident if it ever occurs.

How to Give Criticisms without Hurting Their Feelings

You have genuine intentions of helping them by giving an honest feedback, but you're afraid they might get offended. Here's how to resolve it...

1) Turn it into a lesson.

If your child has done something wrong, never criticize him for his mistakes. Instead, ask him, "That didn't turn out to be ok, did it? What lesson have you learned?" or "That was a great learning experience. What would you do differently in the future?"

Making him realize the moral or lesson to be learned in every failed experience will enrich his character and knowledge.

2) Use a third party or proven facts.

Don't say, "I think it may produce unsatisfactory results if we continue with your plans." Instead, say something like, "Although your proposal sounds excellent, everyone who has already followed the same plan you're proposing right now haven't yet achieved their desired results."

3) Make a sandwich.

Sandwich your negative comment between two positive remarks. Let's say your best friend Paul is going on his very first date. He's all excited and raring to go. Now Paul doesn't have any fashion sense. He's wearing a bland shirt and old jeans. You know all along how he hates to admit that he's wrong. So what will you do to save Paul from an embarrassing first date?

Well, you can first point out the things that you like in his overall appearance. Comment on his well-groomed hair. Tell him he looks cool when wearing his sunglasses. Ask him where he bought his perfume because it can certainly attract women like bees to honey. Be sincere and honest.

Then, insert your advice in a nice and suave manner. You can tell him something like: "Your shirt seems to be very comfortable to wear, Paul. Since this is your very first date, I think Sandra (his date) will be more impressed if you wear something like the outfit that you wore on my birthday. You look smashing when you put on clothes like that." Tell him that you're saying this because you only want him to have the best date of his life, because you truly care about him.

Afterward, make another positive statement. You could say something like: "You would definitely make a big impact on Sandra. She would fall head over heels over your gorgeous looks and happy personality. Have a great time on your date, Paul."

Do you think Paul would be offended by such pleasant comments? Not a chance. You have wittingly inserted slightly negative feedback into a bunch of acceptable and ego-boosting remarks.

4) Replace "but" with "and."

The word *but* may trigger a negative reaction because it sounds like you are counteracting their proposal.

The word *and* sounds like you're adding or complimenting their suggestion.

Example:

*"Mark, your proposal sounds amazing. We'll be able to satisfy the employees and generate more sales. **And** it may entail a bigger budget that seems a little out of our reach."*

You first acknowledge Mark for all the benefits of his proposal (that it will be able to satisfy the employees and create more sales). Then you wittingly mention the objection at the end (that it will necessitate a larger budget, which the company may not approve).

The second sentence begins with *and* not *but* so the objection is perceived to be more of an additional comment rather than a criticism.

5) Relate your story.

Let's say you're the manager of a sales department. One of your personnel, George, has not been very productive lately. You see the flaws in what he's doing. You could say something like, "George, I've been in this kind of situation before, even worse than what you're dealing with right now. So I decided to make more cold calls. I also tried to use strategy X and it worked like a charm. Try it out and I'm pretty sure clients will come rushing in."

George is more likely to be receptive to your advice because instead of criticizing him, you humbled yourself. You encouraged him to do better because you instilled in him the confidence to overcome the obstacles in a similar or worse situation. And you did it with class. He pictured you not as a punishing boss, but as a mentor and friend.

6) Get everyone involved.

This is most applicable when you've unintentionally said something that you immediately regretted afterward. If in the heat of the moment you said, "You're so annoying" to someone, immediately add the words *"...as well as everyone else around here."*

The important thing is to make the person feel that he is not the lone subject of the criticism. This way, you would minimize the personal impact on one person and spread it to everyone else.

How to Get Feedback Criticism

Most of the time, we don't like people to criticize us. But there are certain times when criticism can be a good thing. Like when we need to get feedback to improve a certain aspect of our life, or when we just want to know how much they really like (or dislike) something.

Let's say you want to know if your mom likes the food you cooked. You could ask her, "Mom, did you like the turkey dish I cooked?" If she said, "Yes, it was delicious," you could ask her, "What can I do to make it the *best* turkey meal ever?"

Or let's say you and your friend went shopping. You bought some clothes, but you're doubting if your friend likes your new wardrobe as much as you do. Even if your friend said she likes it, you could further ask, "What would you have bought if you were in my shoes?"

These questions do not reject or overshadow their "opinion" that they like it (whether it's the truth or they just want to please you), but you still get to know their true feelings and even get some important feedback in the process.

How to Dismiss Advice without Offending Anyone

Some people are happy to give advice; they feel like they are contributing something helpful in their own little way. But the problem starts when the recipient of the advice doesn't follow it or has another idea. The adviser might get offended because he will feel that his advice is not being valued. Here's how to dismiss someone's advice without hurting his feelings.

1) Show your appreciation.

Tell the person how much you appreciate his advice, and that you will give it some serious thought. Even if you will not really follow his suggestion, the act of merely considering it is enough to show your respect.

2) Reserve the advice for potential future use.

After a day or two, tell him how his ideas could be of great help or use, but you have also found that it is not suitable to your situation right now. But since you think it's highly beneficial, you will keep it in mind for potential use in the future.

3) Build up the ego.

To build up his ego and make him feel that you respect his suggestions, ask for his advice on another subject; but this time, you tell him you're asking his advice because you're trying to help a friend or relative.

(No need to give any name. If he insists, pick someone he doesn't know. This way, he won't be able to track if his advice was actually followed.)

Summary Outline

I. To build happy relationships, we must be able to handle and give criticism - as well as advice - in the most positive light.

II. How to Handle Criticisms Without Losing Your Cool:

   A. Clarify the details.
   B. Reframe the criticism.
   C. Use fogging.
   D. Apply negative assertion.
   E. Reverse the roles.
   F. Counter the criticism.

III. How to Give Criticisms Without Hurting Their Feelings:

   A. Turn it into a lesson.
   B. Use a third party or proven facts.
   C. Make a sandwich.
   D. Replace "but" with "and."
   E. Relate your story.
   F. Get everyone involved.

IV. How To Get Feedback Criticism:

   Ask questions that don't reject or overshadow their

"opinion," but on how to make it better.

V. How To Dismiss Advice Without Offending Anyone:

    A. Show your appreciation.
    B. Reserve the advice for potential future use.
    C. Build up the ego.

7

The Secrets of Handling Difficult People

In a perfect world, you get along with everyone. Your boss likes you. You get along with your brother or sister. Your neighbors respect you. Your colleagues admire you. Unfortunately, this so-called perfect world doesn't exist. Instead, you find yourself living around or working with people who make your life a living hell.

Such people may include those who disagree with anything you say, the negative thinkers who suck the life out of you, the rude or hot-tempered folks who treat you like trash, or those you simply can't get along with. The worst part is, you have to see them almost every day!

But you don't have to live in agony any longer. This chapter reveals secrets that help you get your way with these difficult people.

8 Ways to Deal with Negative or Rude People

1) Take control of your feelings.

If you let your angry feelings control your actions, you might just end up saying something you'll regret later on. Worse, your stress level skyrockets and your health plummets. So just stay calm. Focus on your breathing and don't let the negativity get to you.

You don't have to raise your voice to make a point; you can smoothly share your point of view or your side of the story by using a well-modulated voice and steady eye contact.

If someone tries to shake you off your footing with their words, smile. Smile and act like you're in control of everything. Always maintain an image of control even if you don't really feel it inside.

If you find it challenging to control yourself, keep yourself detached. Whatever that person does or says, don't take it to heart. Put on a poker face.

2) Tell them nicely how you would like to be treated.

Some people think they can get away with treating you poorly. The trick here is to take charge of the situation. Tell them (in a nice way) that you would really appreciate it if they treat you better.

When somebody - for example a messenger - rudely tells you to pick up your package by the lobby, don't respond in the same heated manner. Instead, smile and thank him for informing you. Then tell him that you'd really appreciate it if he talks to you in a nicer way next time.

3) Use the *"When you..., I got (or felt)... because... Is it ok if you...?"* formula.

Using this format, you can make someone realize his fault and how much it has affected you, as well as persuade him to change his ways.

Example:

When you acted like a crazy person at the party, *I got* humiliated *because* everyone perceived our family to be highly disrespectful. *Is it ok if you* don't do that again in the future?"

If he commits the same act again, simply repeat your statement in a slightly modified way. Let him know that you're not joking around and that you really intend to change his attitude for his own benefit.

4) Seek an authority.

Sometimes, the best way to deal with difficult people is by getting someone else of higher rank (someone they respect or look up to) to talk to them. However, make sure that you tell the "authority" exactly what the problem is and what change you would like to happen.

In a school setting, you can talk to your teacher about it. If it's a relative or a family member, find someone whom that person respects or listens to, and then ask for his help.

5) Steer negative people in the positive direction.

Sometimes, people don't realize just how negative they're being. If you feel that someone is being a little too negative, encourage that person to say something positive instead.

Example:

Uncle Lester keeps rambling on and on about how awful the new community center is. You can ask him to share what he liked about the old community center before the renovations and some of his happier memories there.

By letting him relate something positive to you, you're shifting his mood and thinking from pessimistic to optimistic.

6) Acknowledge your flaw, provide a valid reason, and give a counter offer.

Let's say your family is complaining that you're not giving them enough attention. You're always the first one to leave the house and you don't come back until late at night because of your job.

Tell them, "I know I have been staying out late and I have not been able to take you out. The workload is just enormous. I have to meet strict deadlines so that I may be promoted to give all of you a much better life. Tell you what. After my project is finished, we'll take a vacation anywhere you want to go. Would that be okay?"

7) Focus on your own energy.

If someone is being negative or rude, that doesn't mean you have to sympathize with him at all. Focus on what needs to be done rather than the person itself. You'll be too wrapped up in your goal that you won't have time to be affected by somebody else's mood swings.

Example:
You're excited about a company project but your co-worker is complaining to you about the added workload, how much he hates working here, etc. Don't let him zap your enthusiasm. Instead, concentrate on how great this opportunity is going to be for you and for the company. The more you focus on yourself, the less affected you'll be by negativity.

8) Avoid further interaction.

Sometimes, people just don't like to change or won't give in... no matter what you do. If all else fails, do what you can to avoid being with them. If this is not possible, keep your interactions to the bare minimum. If you have to communicate with them, keep it short and sweet.

Sometimes, you have to prioritize your own health and sanity over other people's inferior treatment. If they're not willing to change for the better, then it's their problem and you don't want to have anything to do with it.

How to Handle Difficult Customers

Everyone knows the policy, "the customer is always right." Unfortunately, the most difficult ones make it a point to rub this in your face. So how exactly do you alleviate the fury of a buyer who is livid because of something you, the service, product, or your company failed to perform?

Because the field of customer service is not a walk in the park, there will be times when you are shouted at, or even hurled harsh words by clients who aren't satisfied. Don't be alarmed. This is a normal situation. And being so, there are ways to rise above it so that you don't break down, too.

1) Get to the root of the problem.

Find out what the client is angry about. Is he complaining about your service? Is he unclear about certain points in the agreement or the product? Did the problem come from you or did it spring out of his frustration over something he misunderstood? What are his sentiments exactly?

You can find out by being calm with the client, no matter how irritable he is. Ask the client to explain the situation to you. Don't interrupt and try to defend yourself, nor correct him while he's explaining. Wait for him to finish before thinking of the possible solutions to his problem.

Ask the customer how he wants the problem to be resolved. If the problem is simple enough, don't say anything more that will upset the customer. Your goal is to solve the problem and get away from the difficult customer as quickly as possible, without sacrificing your business' reputation.

Difficult customers who leave with a bad experience often make it a point to blab about it to other people. And you know how powerful word-of-mouth is.

2) Smile and be accommodating.

Smiling confuses people. Not only does it keep the situation from becoming too tense, it also helps you keep up a cool front. Being charming, friendly, and accommodating often alleviates the problem instantly.

Warning: Be sensitive to people's emotions. A genuine smile is nice, but an insulting smile isn't. So do what you can to resolve an issue and accompany it with a smile. But don't smile while he's giving you a piece of his mind. You need to express your empathy, and not make him feel you're mocking him.

3) Let him know that you understand him.

Building rapport with your client is one of the best ways to get into a straight conversation with him without the flare-ups. This means adopting his current mood. If he's angry, let him know that you understand his feelings. If he is frustrated, empathize. Clients appreciate people who feel their pain. When you do this, you can expect to have a much calmer discussion right after.

Don't say something like "I'm sorry for that. I'm already on it." Instead, say something like "I understand that you're angry now. I would feel the same way if I were you. Rest assured that I will do everything in my power to correct this matter as soon as possible. I will constantly update you of the developments as I progress."

Handling an irate customer is not so difficult if you know how to level with people. Think of it this way. If you were in his shoes, you would be feeling the same way, right? How would you want the other person to face you then? That should always be your guiding strategy.

4) Assure the client that you're taking steps to resolve the issue.

You need to assure the client that steps are being undertaken to correct the issue, and when precisely this is expected to be solved. One thing clients hate most is continuously waiting for solutions that are not certain to happen.

5) Offer a present.

Make sure he leaves your store in a good mood. If you run a restaurant, perhaps you can offer the customer a free meal. Ensure him that the mishap will never happen again. It's a small price to pay for a happy ending.

How to Make People Doubt and Change Their Beliefs

There will be times when your idea or opinion is different from that of other people, and they will strongly insist on what they believe in.

All people have a distinct set of beliefs and values that have been ingrained into their subconscious since they were little. They consider their beliefs as true and undeniable; hence, they will hold on to their beliefs even if there's no strong proof or evidence supporting them.

For example, your parents believe that being employed at a Fortune 500 company is the best choice for career advancement, and would lead to a life of fulfillment. So they want you to apply for a job with these companies. You, on the other hand, believe that setting up your own business and being your own boss is the way to go. Neither beliefs are true or false; each belief's validity is based on the believer's perception of them. So how do you get them to doubt - and therefore change - their beliefs?

1) Use the power of social proof.

People get cues from their surroundings and tend to get influenced by other people's ideas, decisions, and yes... beliefs. Their desire to "fit in" would cause them to shift from their existing belief to that of the group.

If you want someone to switch from their belief to your own, team up with one or more individuals having the same belief as yours (the more people on your side, the stronger the social proof). You can talk to them about your intention to change someone's belief, and invite them to be with you when you're persuading the other party. Ask them to nod their heads in agreement, or say "That's true" and perhaps explain why, so that the person you're persuading would have some cause to doubt his previous beliefs.

If you can't get people to collaborate with you beforehand, you can still pull this off, as long as there are other people who are part of the conversation. As you go along with your talk, you can say, "Am I right?" or "is that clear?" while looking at other people around you. Out of respect, they will either nod their heads or say "yes" or "uh-huh;" and that will give the impression that they're agreeing with you.

2) Create a common goal.

Some people insist that they are correct about certain information. If you're not sure whether your own viewpoint is factual, it would help to say something like, "Seems like one of our sources gave us the wrong details. We had better find out which one is accurate, or we might suffer the consequences later on." You can also say this even if you're absolutely sure you're correct, as we don't want to hurt anyone's ego or self-esteem.

By saying the above statement, you transfer the accountability of the inaccurate or wrong data to an external factor. Instead of fighting who among you is right, you both cooperated to achieve a common goal – that of finding the correct information.

3) Act like they're not in touch with reality.

If they insist that you should not pursue a certain endeavor, you could ignore it like it's not a valid suggestion; or you could put on a bewildered look on your face (as if they don't know what they're talking about) and smile or laugh (as if you're responding to a joke).

4) Ask for a specific explanation.

Some people believe in something simply because that's what's being said by their parents, friends, church, etc... even if it's not based on facts or there's no reliable proof. But if you ask them why, or ask them to explain how it's true, they can't justify their belief. If they can't find any possible reason for its accuracy, they might just begin questioning their belief's reliability. Ask them any of these questions:

"How did you come to that conclusion?"
"What proof do you have to support your decision?"
"From whom did you get the facts?"
"What is your source?"
"Where did you get that information?"

Examples:

Critic: This project is impossible to finish.
You: How did you come to that conclusion?

Critic: James is a worthless employee.
You: Where did you get that information?

Critic: Foods like these cause cancer.
You: What is your source?

Just remember to do it gently. Be careful not to sound like you're disagreeing with them, because you're not. You just want to be sure you get the facts right.

But what if they can explain it in detail, using any pointless method they can think of? You can't disagree with them, as this will only make them defend their belief with more intensity. Here's what you could do...

Simply accept and respect their views first, saying something like, "You got a good point there." Then justify your own side by providing your own proof or evidence that subtly and clearly shows how weak or unfounded their belief is. To avoid any confrontation, use a third party. You could say that this was based on scientific research or an authority's statement.

5) Change the variables of the belief.

There are times when you simply can't alter people's belief no matter how much you try. In this case, you can change the variables of their belief or appeal to their other beliefs.

Example 1:
If your dad refuses to give you a raise in allowance based on the fact that the economy is weak, you can say that since the economy is weak, all the more reason to circulate the money around and help local vendors make a buck.

Researching the specifics will help a lot. After all, studies have shown that people react more positively when you're able to provide credible sources.

Example 2:
You want someone to lend you some money. His firm belief is that all people should be self-reliant and should learn to come up with their own solutions. Since you can't change this mindset, you can target his other beliefs. How about telling him that if you're not able to get the money, you will lose an urgent opportunity that may never happen again? If he has a belief that we should grab all opportunities that come our way, he is more likely to be persuaded based on that belief (and not the belief that everyone should learn to support themselves.)

Of course, it's very important that you don't come up with lies or make up stories that aren't true. If your reason is strong enough and you present your case compellingly to jive with his belief, your chances of getting what you want increases.

How to Handle Questions that Accuse or Condemn

Sometimes, we go through situations where people ask us questions that accuse or condemn us of negative aspects. In this case, the most important thing to remember is to never get defensive. It will only make you look more guilty. And it will only intensify your tendency to be even more defensive.

Let's say someone asks you, "Why can't you understand what I'm telling you?" If you answer, "I'm suffering from information overload," he'll ask back, "Why are you suffering from information overload? Can't you focus on just the important things?" The more you answer, the more he'll ask questions which will only make you more defensive.

Instead of you answering the questions, turn the tables around and put him on the defensive end... by asking him to explain why he thought that way or how he arrived at his opinion.

What you could do is ask back something like, "How fast would you like me to learn what you're teaching?" If he says, "I expect you to know everything in 30 minutes." Then you could ask him again, "How about 35 minutes; is that too long for you?"

The purpose of this activity is to make him defend his answers, instead of the other way around. What's great about this method is that once you get him to talk about the specifics, and drill him down to explain the nitty-gritty aspects of his opinions, he will have a much tougher time answering. It's tough to answer the difference between 30 minutes and 35 minutes, right?

Now what if he says or asks something more specific, and you know you're at fault? How can you "escape" from replying, where you lose whatever your answer might be? In this case, what you can do is to reply back with a solution-oriented statement.

Let's say your spouse told you that you're an irresponsible father (or mother), and you very well know you've been spending a lot more time with your friends than with your kids. You could say, "I believe what you really want me to do is spend less nights with my buddies and help you take care of our kids, right?" Now your reply is much more acceptable, and you can get the conversation to a good start. And of course, you have to start doing what you've promised.

How to Protect Yourself from Verbal Attacks

When someone starts verbally attacking or badmouthing you, it's easy to get carried away with your emotions and fight back. But resist the urge, especially if the person is getting a bit too violent.

What you could do to stop the attack is to acknowledge his words as true (by saying something like "I agree") and then get out of his sight at once.

If he continues to harass you, then verbally attack or blame yourself in a more severe manner than the way he's treating you. The person wants to hurt your feelings; so if you appear to verbally "hurt" or verbally punish yourself, he would have accomplished his aim and has no further reason to attack you.

Summary Outline

I. Most of us, in one way or the other, live with people who make our life difficult at best - or a living hell at worst.

II. Eight Ways to Deal with Negative or Rude People:

    A. Take control of your feelings.
    B. Tell them nicely how you would like to be treated.
    C. Use the *"When you..., I got (or felt)... because... Is it ok if you...?"* formula.
    D. Seek an authority.
    E. Steer negative people in the positive direction.
    F. Acknowledge your flaw, provide a valid reason, and give a counter offer.
    G. Focus on your own energy.
    H. Avoid further interaction.

III. How to Handle Difficult Customers:

    A. Get to the root of the problem.
    B. Smile and be accommodating.
    C. Let him know that you understand him.
    D. Assure the client that you're taking steps to resolve the issue.
    E. Offer a present.

IV. How to Make People Doubt and Change Their Beliefs:

    A. Use the power of social proof.
    B. Create a common goal.
    C. Act like they're not in touch with reality.
    D. Ask for a specific explanation.

E. Change the variables of the belief.

V. How to Handle Questions That Accuse or Condemn:

    A. Make him defend his answers and drill him down to explain the nitty-gritty aspects.

    B. Reply back with a solution-oriented statement.

VI. How to Protect Yourself from Verbal Attacks:

Acknowledge his words as true and then get out of his sight at once. If he continues to harass you, then verbally attack or blame yourself in a more severe manner than the way he's treating you.

8

Five Masterful Steps to Sell Anything Like Crazy

Many salespeople think that selling is just a matter of presenting a product or service to a prospect and asking him to buy it. But this often results in rejections and even a negative reputation for the seller.

If you want to be a successful salesperson, you need to do some digging and investigation to find out what makes your prospects tick, and how your product or service can satisfy their itch. You also need to carefully craft a sales message and offer that they can't resist. And lastly, you need to over-deliver and build your relationships with your customers so you can continue selling to them again and again.

The five steps below will guide you to explosively blast your sales through the roof!

Step 1:
Know Your Prospects.

As wonderful as it would be to just magically convince another person to share your views, life doesn't quite work that way. You have to know where your prospects are coming from for you to know which angle you can best appeal to. This is the basic rule when it comes to selling.

Know your prospect's values, then relate to him how he will have his most cherished values attained by doing whatever it is you're asking him. Recognize what makes him tick. People value different things. Some value money, some value freedom, while others value happiness in relationships. Whatever it is, know them and persuade people in accordance with their values.

If you want to know what someone values, pay attention to where he spends most of his time. If you want to know what someone is thinking often, just observe his actions. To know what someone's goals or dreams are, see what books or information materials he reads/listens to.

You may also ask them questions like:

➤ *"What's most important to you in (buying a computer, hiring a designer, etc.)?"*
➤ *"What factor made you decide to (move here, buy this cellphone, etc.)?"*
➤ *"What do you value in a (relationship, house, etc.)?"*

Customize your message with their specific personality, values, mindset, and beliefs. To do that, you have to dig deeper and ask them specific details that will reveal more of their inner state.

a. To know their decision-making criteria

You might ask, "How do you make a decision in choosing which plan to push through?"

If they answer:

o **"I just know it deep inside."** - This means they rely on themselves, so you can customize your message by saying something like, "You probably already know deep inside that this product is the perfect choice."

o **"I ask the opinion of Mr. X" or "I do research on**

reliable books." - This means they rely on others, so you can craft your proposal by saying something like, "This strategy has proven to be the most cost-effective based on evidence gathered by Mr. X's group."

b. To know if they have the "need" or the "opportunity" mindset

You might ask, "Why did you apply to work as manager in this corporation?"

If they answer:
- **"I need the money to pay the monthly bills."** - This means they are motivated by their needs and less likely by what they truly want in their lives. They are likely to stay in their comfort zone, so words like "having a safe, secure job" are heaven to their ears. You can't motivate them by describing how terrific their future will be because they are tied to satisfying their current needs.
- **"I love the opportunity to meet new people and take on exciting projects."** - This means they are motivated by their expectations of something great or exciting to occur in the future. You cannot motivate them by suggesting they *need* your product or service.

c. To know if they focus on getting pleasure or avoiding pain

You might ask, "Why do you want to become a millionaire?"

If they answer:
- **"I want to travel around the world and buy anything I want."** - This means they are going after pleasure, so you can customize your message by saying something like, "Our course provides you with the opportunity to

go to exciting destinations, meet successful people, eat at the finest restaurants, and shop to your heart's delight."

- **"I don't want to suffer from poverty and constant worrying of where I will get the money to pay for the bills."** - This means they want to avoid pain, so you can craft your message by saying something like, "With this new equipment, you'll never have to experience the agony of stressful labor."

d. To know if they are detail-oriented or the "in-a-nutshell" type

You ask, "Shall we proceed or would you like more details?"

If they answer:

- **"Let's get right to it."** - This means they want the big picture, and they don't want to burden themselves with knowing every specific detail of your product or service. They think and act quickly, so you can persuade easily by simply emphasizing the main benefits and getting straight to the point.
- **"I'd like to study your proposal first before making my decision."** - This means they want to know all the facts, evidences, instructions, or details before jumping into any conclusion. They are prone to analyze and be meticulous with details, so you can persuade them by giving them full documentations.

When persuading anyone, remember that you should always state your message in terms of their specific values and mindset. Remember that they are always asking, "What's in it for me?"

Step 2:

Know Your Product and Niche.

Learn as much as you can about the product you're selling. That way, you'll be able to answer any question they might throw your way. Knowing your product's strengths and weaknesses also helps you persuade them to buy from you.

Think ahead of any possible objections they may have and prepare the solutions in advance. If you're not confident enough in whatever it is you're selling, you don't stand a chance at persuading anybody. So to be a persuasive salesperson, you have to know the most intricate details of what you're selling because prospects are going to be asking a lot of questions about it.

Even if you're only selling a certain type of product, you have to know exactly what you're offering and be well-versed in your field. Study other related products as well, so you can make a good comparison between yours and theirs, and provide proof of how yours is better. Prospects wouldn't want to buy from someone who has insufficient knowledge over his niche, or someone who is doubtful over what he's selling.

Step 3:
Craft Your Sales Message.

When creating your sales message, make the prospect feel that who he currently is - or what he currently has - is not good enough. It is now your duty to let him feel the agony of staying at his current status. Make him visualize the undesirable outcome for not making any change in his life. Here are some clever ideas in crafting your sales message:

a. Use motivational triggers.

If you can craft your message in a way that it appeals with one or more of the triggers below, you are more likely to get better results.

1) Desire for pleasure
2) Fear of pain
3) Having/saving more money
4) Prevention of loss of money
5) Attainment of excellent health and long life
6) Enhancement of relationships
7) The need for love, respect, security, recognition, and trust

Probably the biggest motivators are pleasure and pain. Make him feel the pleasure of doing what you want or experience the pain of not doing what you want. Between pleasure and pain, the avoidance of pain is much more of a motivator.

If you decide to use the pain trigger, paint a clear picture in your prospect's mind of the negativity, consequences, or bad effects of not having your product or service. Ask him to imagine that worst picture in his mind.

For instance, if you're selling life insurance, you could say, "Imagine if something unexpected happens to you and your family has no one else to turn to. They would be forced to go out on the streets, or beg for mercy, or take any job that they could get no matter how hard it is. It would be a nightmare to say the least."

Then after he has realized it, identify the most beneficial aspects that your life insurance has to offer. You can then say, "For only $24 dollars a month, you could have peace of mind and absolute assurance of financial security, no matter what happens. Your family would have all the support they need; and you can always sleep well at night knowing that they will never have to struggle with life's hardships."

As much as possible, show a more emotionally powerful benefit. If you're selling a liquid cleaner, don't just say, "It cleans effectively." Say something like, "It saves your children from having to experience the harmful effects of disease-causing germs."

Most people respond better to emotions than logic. In fact, research suggests that we rely on our emotions most of the time when making decisions. Therefore, you should aim to expound more on your product's/service's benefits (which appeal to the emotions) more than the features (which appeal to logic).

To point out the benefits of your product, show your prospect how it could make his life easier or solve his problem if he owns or uses it.

Feature: This drink contains catechins.
Vs.
Benefit: This drink prevents the growth of cancer cells.

People are afraid to make changes in their lives. They would rather stay with their unsatisfying state of living rather than risk having to lose anything. They foresee the negative consequences of their actions, but not the positive. So make them aware of the negative effect of their inaction. If they can picture the pain that comes along with being stagnant, they will be motivated to take the necessary action to avoid any suffering.

Make them realize the negative end result of staying where they are, then knock them down with the most attractive benefits of your product that will solve and end their dilemma.

b. Divulge your minor weakness or negative point.

Sometimes when we list down ONLY all the good qualities of a product, people may tend to be skeptical or doubtful of what we're saying. To counter this, mention a flaw or bad side of your product before offsetting it with the many good sides. As long as the imperfection is trivial, and your positive features overshadow your competitors', this technique can skyrocket your earnings.

The reason for this is that when you "confess" the negative part, your prospect's defenses will drop down; hence, he will be able to focus on the positive aspects and be more open to accept your message. He would also want to return the favor of honesty you've given to him. By being honest, you've just shown him you can be trusted; he will repay that trust by buying your product or service.

Another benefit is that you establish yourself as an expert who is willing to reveal the bad points, even if it means abandoning your self-interest for his sake. Once he knows you can be trusted and he purchases your item, he will tend to continue trusting and buying from you as long as you continue to meet his expectations.

The Avis campaign of "We're number 2, so we try harder" demonstrates how to use a weakness to your advantage and skyrocket your sales. Within a year of using that slogan, Avis went from losing $3.2 million to earning $1.2 million!

c. Leave the prospect hanging and hungry for more.

According to wikipedia.org, the Zeigarnik effect states

that people remember uncompleted or interrupted tasks better than completed ones. How do we apply this in persuasion and sales?

Keep them hanging in suspense that they will not stop until they know the ending. TV and radio programs use this often to make the viewer stay tuned to the next episode. Copywriters are also doing this to make people continue reading until the very end. They use words such as:
- "**In a few moments**, I'll show you the right way to meet Mr. Right."
- "**In due time**, I'll reveal the answer to this mysterious puzzle.
- "**Soon**, the truth will be revealed!"
- "**Ultimately**, your prayers will be answered."

These words will make your prospects "stick" with you until they've found the information or thing you've been keeping from them.

If you're selling an information product, you can use this effectively by giving them a sample excerpt that ends in such a way that they will want more details from you so badly, they'll have to buy your product to satisfy their urge or curiosity.

The power of the Zeigarnik effect comes from the desire of people to finish what has already been started. Let's say you're a sales manager and you're giving a $500 bonus incentive to anyone on your sales team who could sell at least 50 units per month. To apply the Zeigarnik effect, you could give them credit for 10 sales at the start of the month, so all they have to sell are 40 more units to get the incentive. This motivational push will give them the momentum to "continue" the process. And the closer they are to reaching 50 units, the more inspired they are to attain that goal.

d. Provide compelling testimonials.

Testimonials are very persuasive because they come from 3rd parties. Anyone can make crazy claims regarding how good their products are, but testimonials provide some kind of proof that verify the actual effectiveness of the products... because they're coming (and should be coming) from people not related to the seller.

So collect testimonials from satisfied customers, and use them every chance you get. But above all, never create fake testimonials because it's not only unethical, but will put your reputation at risk. Always ensure that your claims are all truthful and verifiable.

To encourage customers to give testimonials, give away something valuable in exchange for their testimonials. Some of them might get intimidated with writing whole paragraphs, so you can tell them to simply "jot down a few notes."

Let me give you a list here of the most effective types of testimonials to skyrocket your profits.

Success Story Testimonials

An effective testimonial involves a story or case study on how your product or service has improved the life of a person. Use before/after case studies if possible. It's not enough to say, "I love this product!" or "I think this is going to work well for me."

A powerful testimonial includes actual, specific results gained from using the product or service. Here's an example:

"John's fat-loss shake has helped me lose 17 pounds in just 2 weeks! I started taking it last July 2. I was very fat by then. On July 16, my waistline shrunk by 5 inches and I can even see some ab muscles. Thanks for bringing my confidence back!"

Couple the testimonial above with "before and after" pics, and you got a winner!

Authority Testimonials

A testimonial multiplies its power when coming from someone famous or an authority, especially if he belongs to the same field as that of your product.

Testimonials from specialists or popular people tend to gain more credibility and trust, and people associate those aspects to the products being sold.

Sensory Testimonials

The more senses the prospect uses, the more effective the results are. Written testimonials rely only on the eyes of the prospect, and can easily be manipulated. Audio testimonials are more "genuine" since the prospect can actually hear and feel the emotions of the happy buyer.

But nothing could be as real - and as believable - as video testimonials, because the prospect is using 2 senses (eyes and ears); he could actually see and hear (and even connect with) the satisfied customer praising your product.

Doubt-To-Certainty Testimonials

If the prospect could relate to the testimonial as if he's experiencing the testimonial giver's past situation, then he's as good as sold.

The testimonial tells about the frustrating problem the user had, and how he's full of doubt and skepticism in buying the product. But he had made a bold decision to purchase the product because he can't stand the pain any longer. And behold! It dramatically changed his life, and it was the best decision he had ever made.

When requesting for testimonials from past users, ask them to state the problem they previously had. Ask them if they had any doubts in ever buying the product before, and how their decision finally solved their dilemma. Request them to jot down these very crucial details.

Here's a secret method to get "perfect" written testimonials from past users:

Some people are too lazy to write a testimonial (and even much lazier to record one in audio or video format). So you could do it for them. Ask their permission if you could write down a testimonial for them, based on the results you've seen them get. Once you have the "ok" sign, write down a benefit-filled testimonial, and give it to them for editing and approval. They'll either make a few changes or be fine with what you've written. This isn't deceptive, since the customer could change the testimonial and they have to approve it before you could use it.

e. Let your prospect "own" the product before buying it. (Optional)

People would rather not get a thing that they haven't owned yet, than lose something already in their possession. Once they possess something, they treat it with value. So how do you get your prospect to sense ownership of your product, so that he may feel its value and make sure he's making the right decision?

The "bring it home" technique works like a charm. If possible, let him take home the product and use it for a certain number of days. Give him an unconditional guarantee that he can return it anytime he likes. You may either have the option of asking him to pay for it and just refund the money if he wants to return the product, or let him know that he doesn't need to pay anything unless he's really sure that he wants to continue "owning" it (in this case, make sure you get his address and contact details so you can get the payment after the specified trial period). Once he gets his hands on it, he'll be very likely to keep it.

If you are in the computer industry selling genuine spare parts and you encounter a difficult client, come up with "test drives" promo or other noteworthy gimmicks to prove your worth. Through this, the client will know you are a legitimate business worth venturing into.

Step 4:
Present the Offer

To present an irresistible offer, the value of the product should be much more than its perceived price. When the product or service you offer has no standard or suggested price in the marketplace to base on, you can command any price you want. Obviously, it must be something very extraordinary and different from the others.

But if you're selling an identical product or service, you can still ask for a high price by increasing your perceived value first, then offering them a discount.

Let's say you're a good writer, and you're clueless on how much to charge your clients. Some writers charge as high as $50 per short article, while some charge as low as $2! You don't want to charge anywhere within the range of $2 since most will think your quality of writing is bad. (Isn't it amazing how we judge people or things based on the price offered, even if they haven't delivered yet?) $50 per article might be too high though. But would $25 be a reasonable amount? It could be; and although some may still not afford it, you have set your value in their minds. And this is the key: from then on, you can give them a "highly discounted" price of let's say $10. For many, $10 is still too high a price; but with regards to your offer, they would be more receptive to it because they're getting high-quality articles worth $25 each for a bargain price of only $10!

Aside from the price, you may also increase the perceived value by including better versions or bonuses to your main product. For example, you could create an audio version or video version, include worksheets, and add other complementary products. Since many marketers are too lazy to come up with an audio or video version, that's another edge for you.

Another way to boost your perceived value is to limit your availability or imply that your time is scarce. In our writer example, you don't want to sound too desperate and too eager to get them as clients. You don't want to look like you're doing nothing and simply waiting for clients (in their minds, not getting clients means your writing is not up to par). What you could do is subtly accommodate them, but tell them you will get back to them ASAP after you have checked your schedule because you have a line-up of orders and you don't want to take more than you can handle. Or if you can't afford to risk having the client slip away, you can tell them that there might be a slight delay in the fulfillment of their order because you have lots of orders coming through and you want to give each article the necessary attention and time it deserves to ensure its quality.

Another effective strategy is to give out discount coupons. People associate discount coupons as a way for them to save money, even if they provide no significant savings at all. People don't want to analyze the intricacies of things; their time is much too important. A discount coupon would give them a sense of relief because it is automatically perceived as a way for them to save money, time, or energy.

But what if the prospect can't afford the product or service? In this case, it helps to be flexible and have a payment program in place, where he can pay in installments.

Once a prospect goes into buying mode, he is much more likely to spend more with you at that point in time. So why not take advantage of the situation and offer them an upsell or cross-sell?

An upsell is usually a better, upgraded or more expensive version of your product. It could simply be the same item, but with some major features not available in the main product you're selling. An upsell is usually offered before the prospect buys the main product, with the hope that they will compare the upsell with the main offer, and realize that the upsell is a much better deal for the price (despite costing more). If you're selling tickets to a boxing match, you could say, "Would you like to have the ringside seats instead? It only costs $20 more but you'll be so much closer to the action." It could also be a package consisting of the main product and other products that complement it. Classic example: McDonald's "Would you like fries with that?"

A cross-sell is an offer of a related product(s) to a customer. Although it is usually done after he has bought the main product, it may also be presented when they're about to make a purchase. You've probably seen statements like: "People who bought this item also bought..." Those establishments are cross-selling you on products related with the one you just bought. They know that people who are passionate or interested in a certain subject are likely to buy other things with the same theme.

Step 5:
Over-Deliver And Sell More.

Once you've converted a prospect into a customer, strive to over-deliver. After buying it, he will continue to believe (or find ways to convince himself) that he has made the right choice, even if people around him make him realize that he may have made the wrong decision.

However, there are times when people around him might be influential enough to make your customer doubt his own judgment, resulting in what we may call "buyer's remorse."

One thing you can do to assure their satisfaction and minimize refunds is to communicate with the buyer immediately after he has purchased. Say something like, "Thank you for investing in [your product]. You've made a great decision..."

Note the word "investing." It is much more powerful than "buying" or "purchasing" because it connotes that something of equal or greater value will come back in either tangible or intangible form, as opposed to "buying" which has the impression of spending money.

Then by saying that he has made a great decision, you are confirming his belief of making the right move. Think of a time when you know you did the right thing. Having someone else tell you that you made a wise decision makes you more confident in what you've done, doesn't it? The same principle applies in sales.

Start building your relationship with your customer. Give him a free item now and then. Give free personal advice and let him know how to contact you anytime he needs anything. Then as the relationship gets better, take note of his birthday, his sons and daughters, his job... anything about him. Give him greeting cards during his birthday and other special occasions.

As you gain his trust more, you may ask if he could refer anyone to you. He'll be more than glad to! And you'll have an easier time offering him other things you're selling.

If you have various products with ascending price points, you can place a customer in a specific sales ladder. Here's what I mean...

All prospects start from the bottom of the sales ladder. When someone buys, place him in the first rung of your sales ladder. You then make an offer for a 2nd product with a higher price. If he buys it, then you put him in the second rung of the ladder, and offer a 3rd product with a higher price than the previous 2. And so on...

Let's say you're selling a book worth $10. When a customer buys it, you put him in the first rung. All those in the first rung would be offered a CD course worth $97. When he buys the CD course, you put him in the second rung. All those in the second rung would be given a special offer to attend a live seminar worth $297. When he buys again, you put him in the third rung. All those in the 3rd rung would be offered an exclusive, one-on-one coaching session worth $597.

As you can see, the more the customer buys (and the higher he gets in your sales ladder), the more valuable he becomes to you because he'll be more open to buy from you again and again if he is satisfied with his previous purchase experiences.

The key here is to over-deliver on every transaction and make the customer happy and satisfied. As you do that, he will respect, trust, and like you more and more with every purchase he makes from you.

Summary Outline

I. If you want to be a successful salesperson, you need to do some digging and investigation to find out what makes your prospects tick, and how your product or service can satisfy their itch. You also need to carefully craft a sales message and offer that they can't resist. And lastly, you need to over-deliver and build your relationships with your customers so you can continue selling to them again and again.

II. Five Steps to Explosively Blast Your Sales Through the Roof:

Step 1: Know Your Prospects.

   A. Know their decision-making criteria.
   B. Know if they have the "need" or the "opportunity" mindset.
   C. Know if they focus on getting pleasure or avoiding pain.
   D. Know if they are detail-oriented or the "in-a-nutshell" type.

Step 2: Know Your Product and Niche.

Step 3: Craft Your Sales Message.

   A. Use motivational triggers.
   B. Divulge your minor weakness or negative point.
   C. Leave the prospect hanging and hungry for more.
   D. Provide compelling testimonials.

>> >

E. Let your prospect "own" the product before buying it. (Optional)

Step 4: Present the Offer

- To present an irresistible offer, the value of the product should be much more than its perceived price.

Step 5: Over-Deliver and Sell More.

9

How To Make Dog's Mouths Water...

You've probably heard of Ivan Pavlov's experiment where he rings a bell every time he feeds his dog. After some time, the dog would salivate every time it hears the bell ring, even if there was no food. The dogs have associated the ringing of the bell with the food.

There have been reports of weather people being blamed, threatened, or even hurt because people associate them with the bad weather they've reported about, even if these poor weather people have absolutely no control of nature.

Have you ever listened to people talk about their hometown sports team? If the hometown team wins, they say something like, **"Our** team won!" If their team loses, they would probably say something like, **"They've** lost the game." They separate themselves and avoid being associated with the losing team.

Even your kids (if you have them) can influence the way people see you; that's why it's important to teach them good moral values and ethics that would reflect favorably on their parents.

By being related (even in the most minor way) to a person or event, the ego and reputation are affected. That's why you must choose your friends very carefully because the behavior or actions of the people you hang out with can very much reflect on you.

The power of association is not limited to people or

events. In fact, you can associate the quality of anything you can think of with the subject of your persuasion.

Just think about the clothes that people are wearing. What would you think of a person wearing a cross necklace? You would probably think she is religious. You might associate someone in military attire as disciplined and brave, while someone wearing shades as cool.

The Ultimate Weapon of Association

Probably the most effective association tool you can apply is anchoring. In Chapter 1, you've learned how anchoring can power up your belief. In fact, it can help you (or anyone you know) acquire or develop any qualities – confidence, happiness, courage, etc. (to review the steps in anchoring, go to Chapter 1).

You may also use anchoring to help improve other people's lives. The steps are the same but instead of you recalling a certain memory or visualizing to bring about your desired state, you guide him to do just that. Then ask him to tell you when he's in his most intense or peak state, so that you can install the anchor.

Let's say you want to help someone become confident. You could use the power of imagination and tell him, "Imagine yourself walking confidently to your boss and politely asking him to give you a raise..." Fortify the emotion by saying, "The more you picture this scene, the more confident you become."

You could also add past experiences where he showed confidence, saying something like, "Go back to your past and imagine a time when you feel you're on top of your game, when you feel that you can do anything, with nothing holding you back..."

An optional reinforcement would be to tell stories of how someone (less confident than him) has developed super confidence and achieved great results. Your aim is to fire up the intense feeling of confidence from within him.

Then when he tells you he's in his peak state, anchor it.

Want to add a second emotion to the anchor? Sure, you can do that. Let's say you want him to also be persistent. Before firing the anchor, you can ask him to also imagine a past experience when he persistently accomplished a goal, or a scene where he's showing that trait. Just make sure the emotions involved in the anchor are not conflicting with each other. Then after you've successfully anchored it, he will feel both confident and persistent every time the anchor is applied.

But what if you want to use the anchor without their knowledge? Let's say you want Mr. Smith, your boss, to instantly feel thankful every time he sees you. You can't ask him to recall a certain memory (that would be blatantly obvious). What you could do is either wait for the perfect time when he's in good spirits, or you could think of something that would make him feel grateful (you could give him a wonderful compliment or volunteer to help him in his project). Then when you feel that he's in his peak emotional state, fire off the anchor. You could put your arm on his shoulder, pat him on the back, or say out loud, "My pleasure!"

But don't expect an anchor to work the first few times you use it, although it might. You have to make the connection many times before it "sinks in" to the other person's subconscious.

So if you touch your boss' shoulder whenever he praises

you, the anchor might not have been implanted during the first or second time. But when that same anchor has been used numerous times – every time he praises your work – then you could find yourself getting pampered with words of adoration every time you touch his arm!

But how often do you have to use the same anchor to know if it's taking effect? The simple answer is test it! Fire off your anchor; if he doesn't do what you're conditioning him to do, then you need to do it more often.

How to Anchor Yourself to Like Someone You Dislike

I learned this technique from the book "Unlimited Power" by Tony Robbins. Put your hands in front of you, palms up. In your right hand, you visualize the face of someone you like or love very much. In your left hand, you imagine the face of someone you dislike. Look first at the person you dislike, then the person you like. You look again at the person you dislike, then the person you like. Do this repeatedly again and again and as fast as you can. Then put your hands together, breathe deeply and pause for a while. Now imagine the person you dislike. You should like him now or at least your feelings of dislike for this person have dropped dramatically.

How to Make People Like You (or Anything) Through Association and Anchoring

Whenever you want to talk to a person, do it when he's feeling well and in a good mood. That's because he will associate that wonderful feeling with you.

Likewise, if you speak with him whenever he's in a foul mood, he will subconsciously identify you with the negative feelings. When this happens often enough, he might not like your presence (or something about you) without even knowing why.

You can take it one step further by becoming a constant bearer of good news. By relating positive and happy information as often as possible, you'll be associated with good news and good luck.

This kind of idea also works vice-versa. If you're usually the bearer of bad news, then people will unconsciously see you as a dark cloud. You don't want to be called "Bad News Barry" or "Bad News Beth" behind your back, do you? So if ever you have to relay bad news to someone, see if you can find someone else to do it. ;-)

And if you want someone to like something, wait for him to be in a positive state of emotion before showing it to him. By doing this, you're anchoring him to induce good emotions towards that thing.

If you can associate yourself with positive things, then you can also disassociate yourself from the negative ones. How? By referring to the persons or things you've been associated with in the third person (he, she, it, they, him, her, its, them, their, that).

Example:

Leo was meeting his girlfriend's parents for the first time. Things were going well at first until the local news channel was reporting a fraternity fight that broke out between Leo's school and another school. The father knew where Leo was studying, of course, having already grilled him hours before.

"Does your school often get into these fights?" the

father asked.

*"**They** don't really get into fights often. **That** one seems like a solitary case." Leo said.*

Notice Leo used the words **they** and **that**. By disassociating himself from the school, he also got rid of the father's notion of him being a hooligan.

How to Boost Your Sales Using Association and Anchoring

Wonder why many big companies choose famous TV stars to appear in their commercials and not normal people? It's because those stars are famous. They represent wealth, reputation, skills, or popularity. When they endorse a product, you associate that star with the product. Hence, if you like the actor, you will get to like the product. And if you use the product, you tend to feel like the endorser too.

Big companies pay professional athletes large sums of money to wear certain shoes or clothes, endorse their perfumes, drive a specific car, or even eat certain foods. You might be wondering why these athletes are even asked to endorse products that are not related to them or their craft. The reason is simple. As long as the association is positive, it is not necessary that the correlation between the sports star and the product be directly related.

If you can't afford to hire a famous athlete or actor, you could do the little stuffs, like treating potential clients out to a great lunch.

Example: *Hannah works for a large appliance company. Part of her job is to meet with clients left and right. However, Hannah doesn't always meet her clients in the office. In fact, she often* *meets with them in reputable restaurants. They discuss the deal while eating. When the prospect expresses how delicious the dish is, Hannah will subtly insert the benefits of using her products. This is an anchor that will associate the products with the dish. At the end of the meeting, she foots the bill. No matter how expensive the meal is, Hannah pays for all of it (with the company's funds, of course). She wants her clients to feel good about the meeting. She's using the nice restaurant and the delicious food as anchors. Her clients will then associate their good experience with Hannah and the company she works for.*

Although Hannah's company will shell out a little money for the meal, it's nothing compared to the big profits they'll be getting once they get what they want from their prospects. They know that the satisfying emotions accompanied with eating the food and enjoying the ambiance will be associated with the business discussion they are engaged in during the meal.

Here are some more ideas:

1) Donate to charities or sponsor special events.

Giving to charities can associate your company with being generous and sincere. Sponsoring special events such as athletic contests can associate your company with camaraderie, teamwork, and the winning attitude.

2) Find and use hot trends.

Associate yourself, your company, your product or service with the current hottest trends. And you don't have to pay an expensive price to associate yourself with the trends. You can simply put information about the trend in your sales message that associates it with you or the product.

Example: When Harry Potter was trending, one of my promotions was that my product will make them the "Harry Potter" of influence.

Some websites will notify you when new trends or stories emerge. They include:
news.google.com
news.yahoo.com
msn.com
msnbc.com
cnn.com
cnet.com

In order to save time, you may subscribe to their RSS feeds so you may be alerted automatically when buzz-worthy stories arrive. Here's a tool you can use to predict the potential popularity and origin of a trend: http://www.google.com/trends

3) Associate your product with a specific passion.

Associating with a passion is a smoothly effective strategy. But of course, before you do that you need to know their values so you'll have a clue on what their passions are. To know their values, you can ask questions like:
- "What's most important to you about (attending a seminar, ordering a program, etc.)?"
- "What do you value in a (business, car, etc.)?"

Example: You found out that your prospect loves magic, and you're selling a course about how to earn money on the internet. You can incorporate the two themes together so your material can be associated with his passion. You can say something like "This **Houdini** *internet marketing course allows you to* **magically escape** *the rat race by teaching you step-by-step how to earn big profits online in the shortest time."*

4) Make the package identical with the promo.

Remember that a product's package should have the same design, aspects or ideas as the theme of the product's advertisement, so people can make the right connection.

Example: The theme of your ad involves a man driving a Ferrari. Your product package should have that same man driving that same Ferrari. Not another man. Not another car. Not even a different-colored Ferrari.

Summary Outline

I. You can persuade better by associating yourself (even in the most minor way) to a person, thing, or event.

II. The Ultimate Weapon of Association: Anchoring

III. How to Anchor Yourself to like Someone You Dislike: Use the "palm switching" method.

IV. How to Make People Like You (or Anything) Through Association and Anchoring:
Whenever you want to talk to a person, do it when he's feeling well and in a good mood. Be a constant bearer of good news.

V. How to Boost Your Sales Using Association and Anchoring:

A. Donate to charities or sponsor special events.
B. Find and use hot trends.
C. Associate your product with a specific passion.
D. The package should be identical to the promo.

10

The Power of Giving (you're doing it wrong)

When you give someone a gift or do him a favor, that person will want to reciprocate. Society has conditioned us to believe that we must "return the favor." This is the principle of reciprocity at work.

Giving doesn't only mean imparting physical things or doing something for them, but you can also say things that will leave a lasting impression in their minds.

When you give or do something for others, don't ask for anything back just yet (or at least don't make the impression that you'll be asking a favor anytime in the future). If you do, people would think that you're doing the favor because you just want something from them.

You don't want to be viewed as bribing them. What you want is to be perceived as someone who gives unselfishly for their benefit and is genuinely concerned about them.

That's why it is vital that if you have a request or proposal, you do the giving at least a day or two before you ask for something, so that they won't connect the "giving" with the "asking." Whoever gives first has the power to call the shots, but the recipient must perceive it as unconditional.

But what if a long time has passed and they forgot that you did them a favor?

You can subtly remind them of what you've done, but make sure you don't say it directly. Don't say, "I lent you some money when you needed it. I'd like to ask a favor now." Instead, say something like, "How's your Mom? Hope the money I lent you has helped in paying her medical expenses."

Take note that when something you give is perceived as unique or personalized, or when people think that you exerted more effort to do the favor, the value of the gift or favor increases. This, in turn, will also increase your "value" in their minds.

Tip: When someone says "thanks" to you for a favor you've done for him, reply by saying something like, "It's a pleasure. I'm sure you'll also do the same for me, isn't that right?"

By saying this, you just ingrained in his subconscious the need to repay you. Do this in a subtle manner though, as you don't want to be perceived as having a self-seeking motive. Use this every now and then, but not often.

How to Make People Like You Using Reciprocity

People will tend to like you back, if they believe you like them. Even if they didn't like you when you first met, as long as you make them aware that you like them, then they will return the favor.

In fact, research indicates that if they didn't like you in the beginning but slowly learned to like you in the process, they would like you even more than if they liked you already at the very start.

So tell someone what you like about him or how you appreciate his company. Even better, tell a third party (his friend, relative, co-worker, etc.) what you like about the person you're persuading. When the third party tells him what you said, your statement will be treated as more sincere and genuine.

Example:

Jane thinks her co-worker Sarah doesn't like her. Jane could tell Roy (another co-worker close to Sarah) how much she likes Sarah because of her work ethic, flawless presentation, etc. Now when Roy tells Sarah what Jane said, Sarah would be inclined to like Jane back.

But what if deep inside, you really don't like him?

If you just pretend to like him but deep inside you don't, he could sense your insincerity. So what you could do is to list down everything you like about him. Focus on his positive attributes and ignore his "bad sides." Soon enough, you'll begin to like him in a genuine manner (see also "How to Anchor Yourself to Like Someone You Dislike" in Chapter 9).

But don't go around liking someone suddenly in full blast mode, especially if you currently don't have a close bond with him. Do it slowly.

This principle also applies if you want someone to like you (in a romantic way). If you know someone has any feelings for you (no matter how small), let him (and his contacts) know that you're attracted to him. This will magnify his feelings towards you!

How to Improve Your Relationships Using Reciprocity

If you made someone feel that he has been successfully persuading you in the past, you will have better chances of persuading him in the present.

How do you make him feel that he has been persuading you? By simply agreeing with him more often!

You may say something like, "You're absolutely right with what you said" or "You got a valid point. I like your idea" or even something as simple as "Yes, you're right." Remember to convey body language that signals agreement like smiling, leaning forward, and nodding.

Once he consciously and unconsciously becomes aware that you often agree with him, he'll be itching to return the favor.

Example:

Ernie wants his wife Jenna to agree more with his decisions. Now when Jenna expresses her opinion or suggestion, Ernie validates her by saying any of these:
"Yes, you're exactly right."
"You made a good point. I like what you said."
"I couldn't have said it better myself."
"You took the words right out of my mouth."
"I agree with you."

How to Make More Sales Using Reciprocity

If you think about it, the pressure to reciprocate a gift (even something that is not wanted or needed) is so much greater than the pressure to buy something. So what do you do? Give what you're selling as a gift and imply that you're not selling anything but only accepting donations.

Example:
Every year, an institution of partially-disabled artists

would send me a pack of greeting cards "as a gift." They accept "donations"" but they said it should not be regarded as payment for the products; they are simply encouraging the goodness of the human heart.

There are other ways to make more sales using reciprocity. Here are some ideas:

- Treat your prospects to a free lunch/dinner, movie, or show.
- Send them a personal "thank you" mail (handwritten is best!).
- Spread the good word about them (to their contacts, in Facebook and other social media sites).
- Find out what their hobbies are or what they like to do, then give or do something related to their interests. If they're collecting mugs, buy a beautiful mug personalized with their name on it. If they like to play golf, invite them to tee off (your treat of course).

How to Say "No" to Someone Who Wants You to Reciprocate

It's hard to refuse a request by someone who did you a favor. But what if you really can't reciprocate? Or perhaps you just can't do it at the moment?

What you can do is make a counter-proposal so he will feel that you exerted some effort to satisfy his need.

If you don't have any time, you can ask if you can do it later. If it's not possible or if you really don't like to do it, then calmly explain that due to your current responsibilities or time limitations, it won't do justice to commit to something in a half-baked manner. Then ask if another person who is "more available" or "more qualified" can do it, or say that you will see if you can find someone who can fill in or do the job better.

Example:

Joan helped Brian with his assignment. Now she needs Brian's help with her project. Because he's too busy finishing his own project, Brian tells Joan that he'd love to help out but he will fail in class if he doesn't submit his own project on time. Brian tells Joan he can try his best to do both projects, but it will yield poor results because they are so pressed for time. But Brian reassures Joan by calling his other friends and asking them if they can help her out.

Summary Outline

I. When you give someone a gift or do her a favor, that person will want to reciprocate.

II. How to Make People Like You Using Reciprocity:
Make them aware that you like them and they will like you back.

III. How to Improve Your Relationships Using Reciprocity:
If you made someone feel that he has been successfully persuading you in the past (by agreeing with him more often), you will have better chances of persuading him in the present.

IV. How to Make More Sales Using Reciprocity:
   A. Treat your prospects to a free lunch/dinner, movie, or show.
   B. Send them a personal "thank you" mail (handwritten is best!).
   C. Spread the good word about them (to their contacts, in Facebook and other social media sites).
   D. Find out what their hobbies are or what they like to do, then give or do something related to their interests.

V. How to Say "No" to Someone Who Wants You to Reciprocate: Make a counter-proposal so that he will feel you exerted some effort to satisfy his need.

11

Authority: Earn It, Claim It, Show It, Buy It

If you're an expert or authority on a certain field, you're more likely to persuade others, and getting people to agree with you becomes very easy. For one, they already trust your opinion and judgment. And for another, it's not uncommon for people to look for an authority figure to point them in the right direction or guide them to do the right thing.

It's all about credibility. People feel more at ease dealing with individuals who know what they're doing. Or at least, those who seem to know what they're doing.

They also respond well to people who have esteemed positions in their workplace. The psychology behind this is actually pretty basic. When dealing with a stranger, one of the easiest ways to identify whether they are good for you is through their credentials. If you have inquiries about your health, you don't have to actually be friends with the doctor before you decide to consult with them, right?

That's why a request from a manager to an employee to do a certain task will likely get a better response than a request from a co-employee. That's because the manager has more authority. So if you want to persuade, build up your credibility and be an expert/ guru/ authority/ boss in your chosen area of interest.

4 Ways to Be an Authority Figure

Although the most common form of authority is

becoming an expert, or holding a top position or title, there are also some "sneaky" little things you can do to get perceived as an authority.

1) Earn it.

People work hard to attain such titles as doctor, president, general, attorney, professor, CPA, MBA, PhD. This may require a lot of work, time (and sometimes luck) but earning it gives you the best feeling and boosts your self-esteem.

Nowadays, it doesn't take long to earn a reputation. There are many short-term courses that give a certificate or diploma after you've finished the course (which can take as little as a few weeks). Even being able to write an article for a popular magazine or becoming a published author can make you an authority.

2) Claim it.

You can still be perceived as an authority even if you're not an expert on a subject. How? By being the decision-maker!

For example, when deciding where to eat for dinner, you can either be the first to say, "Let's have dinner at X restaurant and then dessert over at Y café," or you can wait until your friends throw a bunch of half-baked suggestions before swooping in with your own. Once they see how decisive you can be (without being too controlling), they'll see you as a "dining" authority and end up turning to you whenever a decision on where to eat needs to be made.

3) Show it.

If you're tall, you're already an authority! Size or height

is commonly associated with power or status. Taller people are regarded as more respectable and intelligent when compared with shorter individuals. That's why shorter people who know the importance of height go to great lengths such as wearing height-enhancing footwear.

4) Buy it.

Things that people wear or use can be seen as a status symbol. People are more likely to be influenced when speaking to a formally dressed person than someone in shirts or jeans. Those wearing expensive watches and jewelries are perceived as powerful and influential.

In short, people may treat you in many ways depending on the clothes you wear, the car you drive, the house you live in, etc. People who are quite insecure with themselves or don't have much to be proud of often resort to buying "status materials" to compensate for their lack of authority since it's so much easier to pay for things rather than earn the title.

How to Be Perceived as an Authority without Being Arrogant

Now there's the rub. You want to be regarded as an authority, but it's not easy letting people know without being perceived as boastful. Fortunately, there are ways you can blow your own horn without being labeled as a braggart. Here they are:

1) Talk about activities or tasks related to your field that will subtly give them hints about your authority image.

Let's say you're a bestselling author. During your normal conversation with a newly-met person, you're discussing what your hobbies are. You could say something like, "Oh, I love writing. And it's a great feeling if your books help improve the lives of many readers. The only thing that drives me crazy sometimes is that my publisher is a little too demanding and wants me to submit my work at near-impossible deadlines."

That will give him a cue that you're a published author, so he'll ask more questions. This time, you can tell him more about your adventures as a bestselling author. You're not showing off, but just answering his questions.

2) Put your diplomas, certificates, awards, trophies, medals, pictures and other things signifying your authority in locations where the people you want to persuade are most likely to see them.

If you or your article has been featured in a magazine, newspaper or book, display these reading materials on a table where people are most likely to pick them up. Or ask them to read your article because you think they'll find it useful (you're being thoughtful here, not showing off).

3) Take advantage of testimonials.

Testimonials are very effective in conveying your authority. Compile all your testimonials and put them on your website (if you have one) or in your materials. Testimonials coming from another authority, especially in the same field as yours, are much more convincing.

4) Request another person to relate your expertise, abilities, or accomplishments to the people you're aiming to persuade.

Recommendations or positive remarks coming from others are more effective because they don't appear to be biased, even if it's obvious that they're affiliated with you. But of course, the more unrelated they are to you, the more credible their statements are.

How to Sell More Using Authority

Here are some ideas to help boost your sales using authority:

- If you're an authority in the product or service you're selling, include your picture and credentials in your advertisements.
- Hire a specialist to represent what you're selling.
- Ask testimonials from satisfied users.
- Give your product or service away to experts in your field and ask them nicely if they're willing to give you a testimonial.

Example:

Jake is selling dental products. If he's a dentist or has any knowledge/experience in the dental field, he makes sure to mention that in his advertising messages. But whether or not he's an authority, he hires a well-known dentist to represent his products. The dentist recommends Jake's items and indicates his approval in the promotions.

Jake also goes out of his way to make sure his customers are satisfied. From them, he asks for testimonials nicely and gives them free items to show his appreciation.

Jake also contacts the top professionals in his field and gives his products away to them as samples. A few days later, he contacts them and respectfully asks for their feedback. Jake thanks them wholeheartedly and assures them that he will repay the favor when they need him.

How to Get Your Way in Relationships Using Authority

Sometimes, the people you're living with just can't see things your way. Or they disagree much more than they agree to your decisions. In this case, you need to "borrow" other people's authorities.

Example: *Your spouse hardly listens to you anymore, but you want him to take your advice very seriously. Now think about the people that he treats with utmost respect. It could be a relative, a friend, or even his boss. See if you can talk to any of these "authorities" and ask him to communicate your message to your spouse.*

Summary Outline

I.   If you're an expert or authority on a certain field, you're more likely to persuade others, and getting people to agree with you becomes very easy.

II. Four Ways to Be an Authority Figure:

  A. Earn it.
  B. Claim it.
  C. Show it.
  D. Buy it.

III. How to Be Perceived as an Authority Without Being Arrogant:

  A. Subtly give them hints about your authority image.
  B. Put things signifying your authority in strategic locations.
  C. Take advantage of testimonials.
  D. Request another person to relate your expertise, abilities, or accomplishments to the people you're aiming to persuade.

IV. How to Sell More Using Authority:

  A. Include your picture and credentials in your advertisements.
  B. Hire a specialist to represent what you're selling.
  C. Ask testimonials from satisfied users.
  D. Give your product or service away to experts in your field and ask them for a testimonial.

V.   How to Get Your Way in Relationships Using Authority: "Borrow" other people's authorities.

12

The Forgotten Art of Comparisons

It's amazing how the law of comparison can make you perceive something to be positive or negative based on the standard it's being compared to.

Let's say you have an average physique. If you're stuck in an island where everyone is extremely ripped and fit, you'll feel a little insecure. But if the people around you are all obese, then you'll feel confident with your figure. Take note that your body didn't change, but your perception about your body changes based on the aspect it's being compared to.

We make our decision or give an opinion by assigning a yardstick that will be the basis for comparing two or more factors.

How to Make People See Things Your Way Using Comparison

You can get your way in relationships when you know how to compare effectively. Here are some clever ways to do that:

1) Complex first, easy one later.

First ask for something more complex or demanding than what you really intended, before asking for your original request.

Example: One day, during a brainstorming session for a project, Bert suddenly had a fabulous idea. He had a feeling his classmates would react negatively to the extra work but because he knew the power of comparison, he made up another idea that is more complex and that required more effort from them all. When the time came to pitch his ideas, he suggested the more complex one first. Naturally, his classmates turned it down, not wanting to do too much. Then, Bert cleverly sneaked in his original idea. Everyone seemed to be more accepting of it.

This technique is powerful because people generally tend to accept something more if they know you tweaked it to their favor. They also tend to compare both ideas; so when the complex one was presented first, the second less complex one seemed easier to do. Another reason is that people tend to comply with a smaller request after they rejected a bigger one (because they feel that you have given them a concession, which they will try to reciprocate).

2) Tell a story.

When you tell a story, you make people's minds more open to accept concepts and ideas that they have previously denied. And they are more inclined to "compare" their status with your story.

Example:

Your friend John is always complaining about his wife's "slowness." She's a good wife, always taking care of the kids, cleaning the house, and cooking great meals; but she's too slow (according to John). They often arrive late in parties because it takes hours for her to get dressed. And sometimes, she takes a long time to cook so John has to wait for minutes as his stomach growls.

Now you want John to ignore the "little" things that annoy him about his wife. After convincing John to communicate openly to her, you tell him a story you heard about how one irresponsible woman had depleted her husband's earnings by playing in the casino all day. This lady also beat her kids cruelly and had no concern for her spouse. In the end, she committed suicide.

When you do this, you make John realize how lucky he is with his wife. Although she's slow, it's a very minor thing compared to the terrible lady in your story.

3) Exaggerate to prove your point.

If you're dealing with a stubborn person, you can "exaggerate" your situation to get his attention.

Example:

You and your business partner opened a business. But lately, he became irresponsible and failed miserably to do his part. You could tell him something like...

"I resigned from my day job thinking that this business we went into will finally free me from the rat race, but it seems I may have to beg from people down the street just to feed my family. I'm on the verge of bankruptcy because of your inaction! Ok, I'm exaggerating. It would, however, help our situation if you can do your part responsibly to make our business successful."

Selling Strategies Using Comparison

Comparing prices in different contexts is one of the most common selling strategies, and below you'll learn some proven ways to present your offer.

1) Offer the highest price possible and slowly negotiate to lower it.

Make a first offer that is "too much to be accepted" yet still realistic. Then present your second "more acceptable" offer after being rejected. People will tend to give in to your 2nd offer if they reject your first one. You can even lower the price further and further as long as you will allow it.

Example: When my wife and I went to Shanghai for our honeymoon, we went shopping at discount stores. When we asked one store owner how much she's selling a particular item, she asked for a very high price. We then negotiated and she gave us a 25% discount. We were not satisfied and about to leave. But then, she slashed 50% off the price! Seemed like a great deal. We thought if we could ask for a lower price, it would be a super bargain. We negotiated once more and after much haggling, the final price was 75% off! We knew that these sellers were applying the law of comparison (wonder if they knew it).

2) Compare prices between two varieties with identical values.

This is especially effective when selling seminar recordings or transcripts. A seminar costs $997, but the seminar speaker decides to sell the seminar recording in a DVD for $97. People will think it's an amazing deal even if it's $97 because they compared $997 with $97 (a big difference!). They'll learn the same information for a much lower price!

3) Shrink a periodic fee down to its daily equivalent.

Membership sites divide their monthly fee into its daily equivalent, then tell prospects something like, "For less than a buck per day, or the price of a small burger, you'll be provided all the training you need to start your food business." Surely, a dollar a day sounds more affordable than paying a price like $29 a month.

4) Same price = fewer quantities + free bonuses

Studies have shown that if you're selling a product in mass quantities, offering fewer quantities of the product at the same price before giving a few more of that same product as free bonuses, can give you a higher percentage of sales (than if you sell the exact total quantities at the same price).

Example: You're selling special pens. Instead of selling 20 pens at $20, you could sell 17 pens at $20 and give 3 pens as free bonuses.

However, it's a different story if the value of the bonuses is dissimilar to the main product. The perceived total value increases if you combine the bonuses together with the main product (as a package), than if you just sell the main product and give the bonuses for free. The reason is because since the value of each item is not the same, the customer could deem the bonuses as worthless (unlike in the pen example where each pen has the same value as the others). However, if you think adding the bonuses to the main product might not be suitable, then you can still sell the main product and give the bonuses separately for free, as long as you assign an amount or value to the bonuses.

Example: You're selling a quality DVD that comes along with a book version and worksheet. You could sell the entire package at $77; or if it's not appropriate, you can sell the DVD individually *for $77, then tell the prospects that they're just in time to grab the special offer - they get the additional book worth $47 and the worksheet worth $17 at no extra cost!*

5) Take advantage of your USP.

Does your product have a USP (unique selling proposition) or a major advantage over your competitor? If yes, briefly explain the features of your rival's products, then discuss the features or benefits of your products that present a significant benefit over theirs. This isn't unethical as long you're not saying anything negative and you're not spreading false information against your competitors; you're simply indicating what makes yours better.

Summary Outline

I. You can make anyone perceive something to be positive or negative, based on the standard it's being compared to.

II. How to Make People See Things Your Way Using Comparison:

    A. Complex first, easy one later.
    B. Tell a story.
    C. Exaggerate to prove your point.

III. Selling Strategies Using Comparison:

    A. Offer the highest price possible and slowly negotiate to lower it.
    B. Compare prices between two varieties with identical values.
    C. Shrink a periodic fee down to its daily equivalent.
    D. Same price = fewer quantities + free bonuses
    E. Take advantage of your USP.

13

The Law of Expectation, And How To Use It

When you expect someone to do what you want, and that person treats you with respect or looks up to you, you have already increased your chances of success.

We aim to meet, if not exceed, others' expectations of us, especially if we stand to gain benefits like getting rewards, earning trust, or being regarded highly. There have been cases where the law of expectation can produce almost miraculous results.

Take the case of cancer patients who were given placebo pills. These are just plain pills that have no healing capabilities. So how did they get well? The power came from their thoughts. They were told that these pills contain the highest amounts of cancer-fighting ingredients that can effectively cure them in a matter of days. They expected to be healed, and so that's what happened.

They believed that their health would be restored. They have registered in their minds that these pills will cure them of their illnesses. In the process, the belief embedded within their subconscious came to reality.

How to Use the Power of Expectation

Here are five powerful techniques utilizing the power of expectation.

1) Use Parkinson's Law.

Want to know how to use expectation to persuade others to accomplish tasks 2 times, 3 times, or even many times faster? If the task requires 3 months to finish, tell them it has to be done within 3 weeks. The magic in this is that the work will be completed in a span of time based on a person's expectation of how much time is required to do it. Parkinson's Law states "work expands so as to fill the time available for its completion."

If they cannot absolutely do it in that span of time, use the power of comparison. Tell them that if they can produce excellent results, they will be given, let's say, a 2-week extension. They will compare the 2 time frames and may even thank you for giving them enough time! You gave them the impression that they are given a lot of time (because you've added 2 weeks to the original 3-week deadline), even when the task can take up to 3 months to finish!

2) Be specific.

Another great tip to maximize the power of expectation is to be as specific as possible. If you can say, "I know you're a fast writer who can turn out at least 7 quality articles within 5 hours" instead of "I know you to be a fast and efficient writer," then the results will be better and more accurate.

3) Find similarities and point that out.

To successfully influence people, find any point of similarity between you and the person you're persuading.

Example: Both of you are members of a reputable association. You can say something like, "As a fellow member of <Name of Association>, I know you want justice to be served at all times. I respect you and regard you as one of my heroes. I'm sure many *people treat you the same. Just want to thank you in advance for continuing the fight to give justice to Mr. Jones. "*

4) Your actions should convey expectation.

Words may not be enough when you're expecting someone to do something. Your actions and body language should be consistent with your oral communication.

Let's say you expect your close friend to go with you to an event. Ask him to go get dressed and tell him you'll wait in the car, then head straight to your car without hesitation or looking for approval.

5) Expect to be expected.

Keep in mind also that people base their expectations on various aspects such as your physical qualities, your surroundings, etc. Everyone will expect a neatly dressed and well-groomed person to be wealthy and successful; that's why it pays to look good when you're persuading others.

If you wear dirty clothes and have unkempt hair, you'll be treated as someone who has bad manners, and they won't expect good outcome from you. The same goes if you have an orderly and tidy home. People will expect you to be an organized person.

How to Make People Better by Expecting It

People act or behave according to how you treat them. When we assign a person certain positive qualities or attributes, that person will allow us to believe that what we said is true.

We act according to how we think others perceive us. An employee who assumes that his co-workers perceive him as incompetent, will probably be unable to fulfill his job well. On the contrary, if that employee thinks that others are praising him for his good work, he will probably produce good results with his job. This phenomenon has a lot to do with his beliefs. What you believe will happen, can actually manifest into reality.

That's why it's important to reinforce people's belief or self-confidence. One way to do that is to remind them of their accomplishments. If they haven't achieved anything significant yet, you may express your "opinion" on how well they're doing their job, how the way they talk reminds you of a famous motivational speaker, how their skills are improving, etc.

So if you treat, let's say, an average student as a genius, and tell him that his performance exhibits that of a highly intellectual person, he will allow us to believe it and indeed become a very smart person. Try it; you'll be tremendously surprised.

If you're a parent, assign positive qualities to your children, even if they don't have those qualities yet. You expect your child to get high grades in school and he will get high grades. You tell your child that he's a bright student, you really expect that to happen, and your kid will meet or exceed your expectations.

Some parents are not aware that they are degrading the self-esteem of their kids by saying demoralizing words such as *"You're not using your head"* or *"This is common sense stuff, and you don't know it"* or *""Jenny (or some other name) is much better than you are."* They think they are disciplining their kids, but they are actually programming them to expect failures and disappointments.

It's very important to be careful with your words. Instead of discouraging them, expect them to be the best they can be. Add the words **"You probably already know"** or **"You probably realize"** in your statements. This is powerful because you're assuming yet subtly suggesting at the same time.

Examples:
- *"You probably realize that you can do anything you put your mind into."*
- *"You probably already know that nothing is impossible with a little determination."*

Presuppositions

Presuppositions assume that the person you're persuading has already accepted your proposal or has reached an agreement with you, even if he has not yet done so.

So let's say you want to convince your spouse to visit your parents sometime soon. Instead of asking, "Do you want to go see my parents?" just ask, **"When** are we going to visit my parents?" Asking your question this way makes your partner think that visiting your parents is already a done deal, and that it is only a matter of time before the trip pushes through.

Here are other examples. Notice the words in **bold** from the examples below.

➤ *"Are you **still** willing to join me in my quest?"* *(Assumes they're willing to join.)*

➤ *"I will give you $100 **when** you finish this task."* *(Notice I didn't say "if" but "when")*

➢ *"**When** do you want to **start doing** your assignment?" (It presumes you will do the assignment; it's just a matter of "when.")*

➢ *"I'm still **thinking if** Friday is the best day to go to Aunt Tina's house. (Friday may or may not be the best day, but you're planting the assumption to go to Aunt Tina's house.)*

➢ *"**How happy** are you to be here in this memorable event?" (It's not asking if you're happy, but what level your happiness is.)*

➢ *"I'm glad you checked out this course. **How** will you **apply** it to your business?" (Assumes you will apply it to your business.)*

➢ *"Shall we start the program on Thursday **or** Friday?" (It's not "if they will start the program," but "if they will start on Thursday or Friday.")*

➢ *"**How satisfied** are you after reading my book?" (It's not asking if you're satisfied, but what level your satisfaction is.)*

➢ *"Have you submitted your application **yet**?" (Submitting the application is already settled. It's just a matter of "when.")*

Presuppositions may also make the recipient assume that something is true or correct, even if there's no evidence to back it up.

Examples:

o *"Do you **know** that this is a very powerful persuasion technique?"*
o *"Can you **realize** how good his writing is?"*
o *"Would you **believe** this special event might not be repeated again? "*
o *"**Fortunately**, you can get the product at a big discount."*

The Magic Question

Make the prospect do what you want right now by asking a question that assumes he has already done your desired request.

Example: *"If you made money with this program, would you continue your membership?"*

If he says "yes," then you're in a much better position to persuade. That's because he will never know if he will make money with your program unless he joins.

How to Get Your Money Back

Isn't it strange how easy it is to loan other people money, yet how difficult it is to persuade someone to give your money back? If you want to get your money back, make sure you include a good reason for wanting it now.

But that doesn't always work, right? In this case, tell the borrower how you appreciate him for always keeping his word; and then a few moments later, ask for the money. He would do what he can to fulfill your expectation of him.

You can also do the 3rd party expectation technique, in

which you tell the borrower that someone (whom both of you know) says that he doesn't expect you will get the money back (get permission first if possible; otherwise, don't name names). This will instill a sense of challenge in the borrower where he'll strive to prove his critics wrong.

Summary Outline

I. When you expect someone to do what you want, and that person treats you with respect or looks up to you, you have already increased your chances of success.

II. How to Use the Power of Expectation

   A. Use Parkinson's Law.
   B. Be specific.
   C. Find similarities and point that out.
   D. Your actions should convey expectation.
   E. Expect to be expected.

III. How to Make People Better by Expecting It:

   Reinforce people's belief or self-confidence. Remind them of their accomplishments, express your "opinion" on how well they're doing something, and assign positive qualities to them.

IV. Presuppositions:

   Presuppositions assume that the person you're persuading has already accepted your proposal or has reached an agreement with you, even if he has not yet done so. They may also make the recipient assume that something is true or correct, even if there's no evidence to back it up.

V. The Magic Question:

   Make the prospect do what you want right now by asking a question that assumes he has already done your desired request.

VI. How to Get Your Money Back:

Tell the borrower how you appreciate him for always keeping his word; and then a few moments later, ask for the money. Tell the borrower that someone (whom both of you know) says that he doesn't expect you will get the money back.

14

The Most Powerful Psychological Trick
That You're NOT Using

In order to be accepted by society, people do their best to stick to their words. It's a matter of honor and integrity. People are committed to doing things that are consistent with their values, beliefs, agreement, or actions.

How to Persuade People Using Consistency

To do this, find out what aspect of your request or proposal could "tie in" with his values. Then relate it to the thing you'd like him to do.

Example 1:
Your brother is a workaholic and you want him to take a break. Ask him if taking care of his health is very important to him. If he says "yes", then tell him that he should take a break from his stressful job and go to a relaxing vacation with you. Saying he doesn't need a break would be inconsistent with what he previously said (that taking care of his health is very important to him). By first asking a question that he believes in or he can relate to, he is in a more receptive state to accept your proposal (which is associated to the question) in order to be consistent.

When someone has made a commitment himself, it is much easier to persuade him at that moment.

Example 2:
A philanthropist has just announced his commitment to saving the environment. Now would be a good time to solicit his help

for your "Revive the Rainforests" campaign. After all, he has just said it himself. Backing out now would tarnish his name.

How to Get Someone to Stay Consistent With His Commitment

It's frustrating if someone has agreed (or promised) to do something, but he doesn't live up to his word. Here are ways to turn this around.

1) Ask for the commitment.

If you want your business partner to attend an event, don't just send him an invitation or tell him to go. Ask him if he can commit himself to go on that special day, or ask something like "So I'll see you there?" and wait for a "yes." It's important that he verbally confirm his commitment.

2) Let him see himself already immersed in his commitment.

You can do this by asking, "What will you wear to the event?" or "Who shall we look for first?" or "What time will you leave your home?"

When he answers any of these questions, he's reinforcing his commitment because he sees himself doing the things that are done prior or during the event.

3) Let him know the consequence of not doing what he has committed to do.

It could be that he could lose out on a huge opportunity, or that you could end up in dire straits without him by your side.

4) Ask him to write down his commitment.

Writing things down takes more effort than just simply thinking about it. People who exert that extra effort have the inclination to value or cherish whatever they've written down. This follows the principle that we value something more if we exert more effort to attain it.

This becomes even more powerful when other people (especially someone with authority) know of the commitment being made. So asking the person to write down his desired seating location, and telling him that you'll let your boss and co-workers know he's coming, can solidify his commitment.

This is the same reason why we need to write down our goals. We tend to stay committed to written goals and when we share these goals with other people, they become even more powerful because it makes us more accountable.

5) Use the foot-in-the-door technique.

The way this works is that you get them to comply initially with a small favor – something insignificant enough for them to do with the least amount of resistance. Once they have complied with that small favor, you'll have a much easier time persuading them to do larger favors.

For example, you can ask your dad if you can attend this concert with a friend. If he gives you permission, you can later ask him for a bigger allowance, and so on.

One important thing to remember in using this technique is that the person you're persuading should think that he agreed to the initial small request voluntarily.

The minor small request can be anything like: "May I borrow your pen so I could sign this paper?" or "Could I talk to you for even just a few seconds?" or even "What a cute puppy. Can I touch it?"

When you begin even the smallest transaction, the momentum starts to build up. Although some people would comply with your 2nd (more demanding) request after they agreed to a first minor one, it's more effective if you ask requests in a gradual manner.

Don't ask if you can borrow a piece of paper, then immediately jump to borrow his new car. Take it easy. Borrow a piece of paper, then his book next time, then his bag, and so forth.

> **Tip:** Did you know when you ask for something seemingly ignorable, you're likely to get much more than you asked for? So if you want to have a good talk with someone, say, "Could you give me even just a few seconds of your time?" This can make the request seem much smaller and acceptable than if you say, "Could you give me a few hours of your time?" Nonetheless, the amount of time he gives you would likely be the same regardless of which question you asked. Big surprises can indeed come from small packages (or requests).

6) Remind him of his inconsistency (if he strays away from his commitment).

If someone who has committed doesn't stick to his words, you can say something like, "You mentioned you really want to go to the event. May I ask why you're deciding to back out now?"

You just emphasized his inconsistency with his words.

He'll feel so uncomfortable with his inconsistency that you might just persuade him now.

How to Change the Minds of Consistent People

Sometimes, you may have difficulty persuading people to change their stance or decision because they have already made up their mind, and they want to stay consistent with it.

It's only natural for people to protect their ego and not be perceived as fickle-minded. One way you could make them change their views - and let them save face at the same time - is by introducing new or extra information. Since this added data has changed the nature or aspects of the situation, they can change their mind and still think they are responding appropriately.

Another way is by helping them weigh the pros and cons of changing. One of the cons could be that they'll have to step out of their comfort zone. However, you should immediately counter that with a pro by saying that the greatest of men have had to venture out into the unknown before they became who they are today.

The cons represent the set of beliefs they hold about change right now, while the pros are your opportunities to get inside their head. Obviously, there should be more emphasis on the pros than the cons; or else, you lose the argument.

You could ask them to remember - or remind them of - any past event or experience when they did something that is identical to what you want them to do or believe. This way, they will act consistently with their past actions.

How to Increase Sales Using Commitment and Consistency

Here are three ways to use consistency and commitment to rocket your sales.

1) Set up contests, promos or special events that highlight your products or services.

Marketers have been staging contests on who can submit the best success story as a result of using their product. Now that's strong commitment put in writing! People (even non-consumers) will be apt to believe in what they've written and continue to patronize the product, because not doing so will make them inconsistent with their written commitment.

2) Give away items that advertise your main products or services.

You can give away t-shirts, key chains, mugs, caps, pens, or any kind of everyday item where your logo and marketing message are written. If you're wearing a McDonald's t-shirt, you would think twice before eating at Burger King, right?

3) Get them to buy at least once.

Sell your products at ridiculously low prices, even to the point of break-even. Your primary objective is not to gain profits, but to get people to commit to a purchase; because once you have turned the prospects into customers, they will be more committed to buy again from you (as long as they're satisfied of course).

Summary Outline

I. People are committed to do things that are consistent with their values, beliefs, agreement, or actions.

II. How to Persuade People Using Consistency:

Find out what aspect of your request or proposal could "tie in" with his values. Then relate it to the thing you'd like him to do.

III. How to Get Someone To Stay Consistent With His Commitment:

   A. Ask for the commitment.
   B. Let him see himself already immersed in his commitment.
   C. Let him know the consequence of not doing what he has committed to do.
   D. Ask him to write down his commitment.
   E. Use the foot-in-the-door technique.
   F. Remind him of his inconsistency (if he strays away from his commitment).

IV. How to Change the Minds of Consistent People:

   A. Introduce new or extra information.
   B. Help them weigh the pros and cons of changing.
   C. Ask them to remember - or remind them of - any past event or experience when they did something that is identical to what you want them to do or believe.

V. How to Increase Sales Using Commitment and Consistency:

    A. Set up contests, promos or special events that highlight your products or services.

    B. Give away items that advertise your main products or services.

    C. Get them to buy at least once.

15

Scarcity: The Value Multiplier

The more scarce or unavailable the item is to most people, the more valuable it becomes even if none of the product's qualities change. Being aware of its limited quantity or availability is enough.

We all hate to lose our freedom of choice. That's why the more restricted our freedom to choose is on a particular object, the more we want to possess it. So beware! Never tell someone he can't have something you really don't want him to have. It will just fire up his desire!

It's therefore no wonder why putting an age restriction on a movie, magazine, or website (ex. For adults only - 21 years and above) just fuels the hunger of those people under that age to access the material. You may also have seen stories of how couples defend their love to the death when their parents actually forbid their relationship to continue. The degree to which something is banned or limited is directly related to its attractiveness and value.

Selling Strategies Using Scarcity

Scarcity creates urgency. When using scarcity as a selling tactic, you should structure your offer in such a way that it creates a sense of pressure for getting your product or service now! This sense of urgency compels them to eliminate distractions and focus on your message, or they'll lose out.

Let them be aware that you have a strict deadline.

P a g e | 151

Highlight the best thing that can happen if they do what you want, and the worst thing that may occur if they don't. Here are 3 ways to make scarcity a powerful selling arsenal.

1) Limit quantities.

Announce that only a certain number of copies will be sold. People naturally want things that few possess. Many sellers use the "limited supplies" or "limited edition" technique where only a specific number of quantities will be sold; once they're sold out, they're gone for good (just make sure you'll actually stop selling them or your reputation will go downhill).

The perfect time to use scarcity of quantity is if you have an updated or improved version of a product you're selling regularly. That way, you can still continue selling a different version of your product while using scarcity tactics on your current version. This is very powerful because if something that is previously unlimited in quantity suddenly becomes restricted or scarce, that resource becomes more valuable (than if it is scarce all along). Once you lost your freedom of choice (when you previously had it) on something, then it becomes more desirable, attractive, and valuable than ever before.

2) Make it time-sensitive.

Use the "time-sensitive" tactic where the offer is good only up to a certain date. Internet marketers use a script on their websites that "counts down" the remaining days, hours, minutes, and even seconds before the special promo finally expires. Another method that invokes the principle of urgency more is the "one-time offer" where you are given only one chance to grab the offer right now, or lose out on the opportunity forever. Take it or leave it.

3) Set up a rivalry.

It's the competition to get a certain item that augments its value many times over. If supply is less than the demand, you can be quite sure that resource is perceived to be of high value.

Sales people take advantage of this knowledge by scheduling a specific time when all interested prospects come at the same time to view a sales presentation for a scarce item or by simply informing them that there are other people on the "waiting list" who are eager to buy it if the initial prospects don't get it now.

How to Increase Your Value Using Scarcity

Scarcity is not only applicable to products. You could also use it to increase your value as a person by making people aware of how precious or limited your time is. You could imply that you're being paid a certain amount per hour, or that you can only devote 10 minutes of your time to talk to them because you have other important projects to attend to.

If you're always available to do something for someone, it's time to re-evaluate the time you're spending and see if you can limit it to increase your perceived value in their eyes.

Summary Outline

I. The more scarce or unavailable the item is to most people, the more valuable it becomes, even if none of the product's qualities change.

II. Selling Strategies Using Scarcity:

    A. Limit quantities.
    B. Make it time-sensitive.
    C. Set up a rivalry.

III. How to Increase Your Value Using Scarcity:
Make people aware of how precious or limited your time is.

16

Body Language 101

Having the ability to read body language - and use it to influence people - is a necessity if you want to be the best persuader you can be. There are many instances where emails or postage mails result in miscommunication because of the absence of body gestures. Although some people could "sense" emotions through written words, it's not as effective as face-to-face interactions.

By interpreting what someone's body is saying, you can decode his inner emotions and thoughts even if he doesn't say a single word; hence, you can adjust your message or behavior according to his present mood or state of mind.

By knowing what certain body movements imply, you can deliberately do more positive gestures and avoid the negative ones. Even if other people don't know how to read body language, they can subconsciously sense if your movements are "right" or "wrong." With this knowledge, you can create a strong impression, build trust, and ultimately persuade individuals to do what you want.

How to Detect Someone's State by Reading His Body

Some people interpret only one body language sign and make a judgment based on that alone. This is a big mistake. Let's say a person is squinting his eyes. You can't jump to the conclusion that he doesn't like what you said. It may be because some dirt entered his eyes, or maybe he forgot his glasses and can't see clearly, or perhaps it's his personal mannerism.

In this case, you should observe clusters of movements. Observe his other body parts and see if he gives away any other signs of dislike or discomfort. Does he also cross his arms, compress his lips, or lean away from you?

You should also be aware of patterns. Does he always squint his eyes, even when he's feeling positive or comfortable? Does he do it only when you ask a personal question, or even when he's having a great time talking? You must consider these things to be able to read people accurately.

Another thing to be aware of is your environment. In a bright room or when exposed to light, the pupils become smaller, while in a dark room, they get dilated. If the person is sweating too much, it doesn't necessarily mean that he's nervous. The hot weather or a medical condition could be blamed.

The more you observe clusters, patterns, and the environment, the better you would be able to accurately decode what his body language is saying.

Written below are clusters of body gestures that manifest when a person feels a certain emotion or goes into a particular state:

1) Interest or Excitement

When someone is interested in you or in what you're saying, he maintains eye contact more than 60% of the time. The more wide-open the eyes are, the more interested (or aroused) he is. His head may tilt slightly or may be inclined forward. His feet may be going up and down with excitement, or pointing towards you. When standing, his legs may be in a crossed position.

2) Openness

When he's more open to agree with you, his head may be inclined forward and you may find him nodding every now and then (nodding is a sign that he agrees with you). If he's stroking his chin, he may be thinking or listening attentively (and may agree with you after careful evaluation). When his arms are initially crossed and he suddenly uncrosses them when you arrive at a certain subject, that may mean he became more open when you touched on that topic. His hands are not hidden in sight. When he's talking, his hands are open and expressive with his palms upward. His legs may be spaced out from each other when sitting.

3) Boredom

When a person is bored, he shows inattentiveness by staring at a blank space or by looking around frequently. He may also be tapping his fingers on the table and/or tapping his foot on the floor. His chin - or one side of his cheek – may be resting on his hand. One foot or both feet may be pointing in the direction away from the person or thing that bores him, as if he wants to get out of the room.

4) Confidence or Power

When a person exhibits confidence or authority, he usually maintains firm eye contact and his chin is tilted upwards. His chest, throat, and stomach are usually projected outwards. He maintains an erect posture. His hands may be interlaced behind his head or placed beside his hips. His hands may steeple (fingers of one hand connect with the fingers of the other hand, like in a praying position except that the palms are not in contact with each other). He usually has a firm handshake, with palms pointing downwards. He moves with precision and with no hesitation, because he is assured of his actions. His legs may be crossed when standing.

5) Anger or Resistance

Blinking constantly, eye squinting, or clenched fists may be seen on people who are angry or resistant. His hands may be tapping on the table and/or his feet may be tapping on the floor. He may use one hand to clutch the other hand, arm, or elbow (as if restraining himself from making a violent move). Arms crossed over the chest may be a sign of resistance or discomfort, especially when accompanied by clenched fists or when his hands are tightly squeezing the arms.

6) Nervousness, Discomfort, or Insecurity

A nervous person may compress his lips (making them disappear), clear his throat, or stutter when he speaks. His eyes may evade you or they may be squinting. He may also clench his fists or grasp something firmly. He has a wilted handshake; his palms may be sweating and pointing upwards. He may fiddle with his fingers, touch his neck or face, or do other blocking gestures such as crossing his arms or putting an object in front of him. He may also just hide his hands. He may interlock his ankles while sitting.

7) Doubt or Disbelief

Someone who is doubting you or not believing what you're saying, may put his hand over his eye or glimpse from the corner of his eye. His pupils may become smaller. He usually leans away from you. He may touch his neck or face. His arms may be crossed over the chest, and his hands may be tucked in the pockets.

8) Concealment

A person who is hiding something from you usually avoids eye contact. He may "block" his body by crossing his arms or putting an object in front of him. He may put his hands in his pockets or behind his back. His ankles may be interlocked when sitting.

Tip: You may have seen "arms crossed over the chest" in many of the states above. The underlying principle in this gesture is that it implies discomfort. The person is trying to appease himself by blocking his body. Someone who feels uneasy may block his body through other means, like putting an object in front of him or play with his fingernails.

How to Detect Lies

When a person is lying, his eyes may blink faster than their normal rate of blinking. He may look somewhere else or glimpse from the corner of his eye. He may touch his face... especially the mouth, ear, and nose as if covering them. He may place an object in front of him. He barely moves his hands and feet, as if they're frozen. His poses are closed, descending, and insecure. He may be constantly moving from one place to another or changing his poses. He may also project parts of his body (ex. feet) to an escape route (door).

There are other advanced techniques you can use to predict if someone is lying or not. I've listed three of them below.

Advanced Technique # 1:
Eye Reading

If you ask a question to a right-handed person (majority

of people), and he looks to the right in an upward direction, that means he's thinking or "visually constructing" an image in his mind.

If he looks to the left in an upward direction, he's recalling or "visually remembering" something that actually happened.

So let's say you ask him, "Where were you when the child fell down?" If he looks up to the right, he might be making up a story to cover the real incident. If he looks up to the left, he might be recalling what actually happened (in reality).

This method may help you determine if you want to accept his explanation or not, while also taking into account other factors. Note that the meaning of these eye directions tend to have the reverse interpretation for a left-handed person.

Advanced Technique # 2:
The Made-Up Story

This technique involves making up an incident that actually didn't happen and then reading his reaction. In most cases, you ask one question at the end to confirm if he's indeed lying.

Let's say one of your maids asked if she could borrow some money. Her story went on that she has a sick daughter and she needs to go to the downtown hospital immediately. You have a sense of doubt, but the kindhearted person in you lends her money anyway.

Here's one way to know if she indeed went to the hospital or somewhere else. You can tell her something like, "I heard over the news there's a fire in the downtown hospital.

Firefighters have spent hours controlling it. Is your daughter safe and far from the fire?" Now watch her reaction.

If her body language shows some tension or discomfort, if she doesn't answer immediately, if she tries to change the topic, or if she talks about your "made-up" story, then you're probably looking at a liar. Because if she's telling the truth, she would have quickly said something like, "Huh?!? Are you sure? There was no fire there the whole time."

The made-up story technique is also useful when you want to know if someone is hiding something from you. In this case, you pretend to ask her advice about a made-up incident that is similar to the subject in question.

Let's say you suspect your roommate, Jane, is the one spreading terrible rumors about you. You can then ask her, "Jane, can I ask some advice? My close friend is at the peak of her career but she got suspended because some jealous co-workers were spreading rumors about her. What do you think she should do?"

Now observe her reaction. If she still feels comfortable (watch out for her body language) and willingly offers you advice, or even just goes on to talk about it, then there's a big chance she's not spreading rumors about you.

But if she suddenly feels tense or anxious, tries to change the topic or becomes defensive ("I will never spread rumors."), then she's probably guilty.

Advanced Technique # 3:
Pattern Checking

The key here is to study the patterns of how someone will react whenever you ask something he won't tell a lie about. For example, you know that he hates a certain political candidate. You can ask him, "Would there be any chance you'd vote for Mr. X?" Observe his facial expressions or body movement before he speaks. Ask other questions that you know will have a definite answer of "no." Now you can ascertain that when you ask a question and he exhibits those movements, he's disagreeing with you (or saying "no" to you).

Here's another example. You found out from his close friends that his dream is to be a doctor. You can then ask him, "Have you ever wanted to become a doctor?" Obviously, you know the answer is "yes."

But you're not after his answer (you already know that). What you're really after is knowing how his body reacts when he's telling the truth or not. So next time when you're asking something that might have a deceptive answer, you'll have a keen sense of whether he's telling the truth by observing his body movements before he speaks.

These interpretations may not be accurate 100% of the time, but they are very dependable. Now you know how someone may feel even if he's not telling you about it. Use this power to your advantage.

How to Persuade With Your Body

Some people relate positively to actions, and your body language should specifically coincide with the words coming out of your mouth. Make your words congruent with your body gestures, as people could "see through" any inconsistencies that might cause them to doubt. Here are some pointers to remember:

1) Matching

Establish rapport by matching the breathing patterns, postures, speaking style, or movements of the person you're with.

2) Eye contact

Establish eye contact often, especially when listening to a question. If you continuously avoid making eye contact, you might be perceived as someone who is insecure, unreliable, or even deceitful. If you're too timid or are afraid to make eye contact, just look at the bridge of the nose or the portion between their eyes, and he'll think that you're looking at him. Avoid wearing sunglasses, because covering up the eyes might give the impression that you're hiding something. Be sensitive to your eye movements. Don't roll your eyes, as this indicates irritation.

3) Blinking

Be aware of your blinking rate. Blinking too much is a sign of anxiety brought about by deception. The normal rate is around 10 blinks per minute, but can be affected by fatigue or other health conditions. If you have a blinking problem due to health issues, it's a good idea to have a check-up.

4) Hand gestures

Let the other person see your hands while you're talking. Use your hands cautiously while talking. Don't make gestures that are forceful or vigorous. Keep your fingers pointed inwards. Don't point - it gives the impression that you're condemning the other party. Avoid fidgeting as it conveys nervousness or anxiety. Avoid putting your hands on any part of your face, as they may sense you're hiding something. Never cross your arms.

5) Spacing

Provide moderate spacing between you and the person you're persuading - about two feet apart. If you're too near, you're entering into his private territory. If you're too far, you will project an impression of being detached and unapproachable.

6) Sitting

Sit in a comfortable, self-assured manner. Don't sit up stiff and straight. Sitting in a rigid form gives the impression that you are tensed and self-conscious. Don't slump in your seat either. Spread your legs apart. Don't tap your feet.

7) Walking

When walking, look straight ahead with your chest out and walk in an upright, moderate-paced manner.

8) Smiling

Smile genuinely and with confidence. Think of positive things about the person you're with. Think happy thoughts or experiences to bring out the genuine smile in you.

9) Touching

Be careful to touch the right person on the right place. Touching is discouraged when the relationship is between a superior and a subordinate. Most males don't have any issues when touched by females on any body part. A man may touch a fellow male on the shoulder, upper arm, or forearm; but he may become uneasy or defensive when touched by a male stranger or non-acquaintance. Most females are receptive to being touched by fellow women.

However, men should be careful when touching females. They may touch women lightly on safe spots such as the hands or forearm, but they should still exercise caution and consider the relationships between them. In his book "The Psychology of Persuasion," Kevin Hogan mentions that the ideal way to use touch is before your key point. He says to use your middle finger and pointer finger to touch the other person's forearm, hold for one to three seconds while establishing eye contact, state your point, and ask for agreement.

10) Physiology Alteration

There are times when you're persuading someone who seems to be hardheaded. He doesn't want to listen to you and refuses to change his mind. In this case, one thing you could do is to alter his physiology. If he's standing up still, try to get him to walk with you or ask him to sit down. If he's sitting down, try to get him to stand up or stroll around. Getting someone to change his body position or move around is a proven way to change his thoughts or views about something.

Summary Outline

I. By interpreting what someone's body is saying, you can decode his inner emotions and thoughts even if he doesn't say a single word; hence, you can adjust your message or behavior according to his present mood or state of mind. By knowing what certain body movements imply, you can deliberately do more positive gestures and avoid the negative ones.

II. How to Detect Someone's State by Reading His Body

    A. Interest or Excitement
    B. Openness
    C. Boredom
    D. Confidence or Power
    E. Anger or Resistance
    F. Nervousness, Discomfort or Insecurity
    G. Doubt or Disbelief
    H. Concealment

III. How to Detect Lies

    A. Eye Reading
    B. The Made-Up Story
    C. Pattern Checking

VI. How to Persuade With Your Body

    A. Matching
    B. Eye contact
    C. Blinking
    D. Hand gestures
    E. Spacing

F. Sitting
G. Walking
H. Smiling
I. Touching
J. Physiology Alteration

17

So... Now What?

Now that you have finished this book, you are ready to go out into the world and start getting what you want out of life. You know how to use the same persuasion techniques used by the top politicians in the world in everyday interactions. But this is just the beginning of the journey to change your life forever.

So to help get you started I have listed below some free courses that I highly recommend which you can download online.

The password to the page is: "Michael Lee"

Assertiveness Maker Hypnosis Audio -

"Assertiveness Maker" is a powerful 17-minute hypnosis recording that will automatically transform you into a highly assertive (yet very likeable) person. All you need to do is just listen for 17 short minutes. That's all!

It will re-wire your inner programming for assertiveness, "install" the vital persuasion and people skills down to your inner core, and skyrocket your success rate!

Price Value: $47.00

Get it at: www.expertpersuader.com/bonuses.php

Confidence & Charisma Dynamic Hypnosis Session -

Confidence and Charisma is about you becoming someone who 'turns-heads' when you walk into a room. This hypnosis session helps you have more confidence to succeed and become more charismatic to carry it off, both socially and in business.

Price Value: $27

Get it at:
www.expertpersuader.com/bonuses.php

"The #1 Ingredient for Success and Happiness in Life Video"
by Dr. Joe Rubino

In this hard-hitting, insightful, hour-long television interview, Dr. Joe Rubino, one of the world's leading life optimization coaches and experts on self-esteem elevation is interviewed by personal development expert Bill Covert.

Dr. Rubino answers questions that encompass the origins of low self-esteem, the emotional addictions that ruin people's lives, the keys to healing one's painful past, the best ways out of the downward spiral of damaging self-talk and destructive interpretations, the secrets to creating an empowering life plan, the antidote to resignation and self-sabotage, the access to designing an optimum life of no regrets that is marked by passion, purpose, fulfillment, abundance, rich relationships, and happiness and much, much more.

Called by many as the most informative and interesting interview they have ever seen, this enlightening dialog will challenge viewers to step into a whole new way of being that reflects their inherent magnificence.

PLUS it comes with a 7-part Self-Esteem Mini Course and Success Club Membership.

Price Value: $129 value

Get it at:
www.expertpersuader.com/bonuses.php

Isohypnosis Attract Good Health

At last, an incredible new way to attract good health by using hypnosis. This is an amazing combination of the Mind Sync 3D Hypnotic Technique® and the scientifically proven Mind Sync Hypnosis Videos® to attract good health quickly, effectively and permanently.

Price Value: $24.95

Get it at:
www.expertpersuader.com/bonuses.php

Ultimate Productivity Mastership

If you feel overwhelmed, then this is what you are looking for. Discover the best way to plan yourself for greatest productivity. This course will show you the best strategies to manage your time.

Value: $27.00

Get it at:
www.expertpersuader.com/bonuses.php

6 Free Pre-made Mind Movies

Get 6 free pre-made Mind Movies focusing on the 6 key areas of life: wealth, relationships, attracting the perfect woman, attracting the perfect man, spiritual fulfillment and health and fitness. Watch your pre-made Mind Movie once in the morning and once in the evening and you'll quickly begin to enlist the help of the Universe to help you achieve your goals and desires faster and easier than you ever thought possible.

Value: $234

Get it at:
www.expertpersuader.com/bonuses.php

Bonus Name: Attract Love Hypnosis Mp3

Attract Love is a hypnosis mp3 program designed to help re-wire your subconscious mind to improve relationships, attract the partner of your dreams and make you open to receiving intimacy and true happiness.

Price Value: $37

Get it at:
www.expertpersuader.com/bonuses.php

Guest Chapter

By: Natalie Ledwell[1]

Are You Skilled in the Art of Authentic Persuasion? Here's How to Find Out:

Persuasion is about so much more than just getting someone to do what you want. True "authentic persuasion" in the way that I define it is about being able to share your point of view or your ideas with others in a way that they feel excited, engaged and on board.

Are you skilled at enrolling other people in your ideas or what you'd like to create?

Here are 3 signs that you may still have some growing to do in the art of authentic persuasion:

Sign #1:
When sharing your ideas, you feel overlooked or ignored.

Have you made several attempts at trying to land that promotion at work, scoring a date with someone special you've had your eye on or enrolling your spouse in a particular idea... but you haven't been successful?

---

[1] Natalie Ledwell is a bestselling author, speaker and successful entrepreneur. She's passionate about helping others to achieve their greatest dreams and ambitions through her personal development programs and her online TV show, The Inspiration Show. Find out more about Natalie and her company Mind Movies by visiting http://www.mindmovies.com

Chances are you need to do a better job at painting a mental picture for them that's compelling enough to make them want to give you the yes you've been looking for.

To change this, focus on sharing what the BENEFIT is to the other person to granting your request. Speak from that place and you'll likely begin seeing more results instead of refusals.

Sign #2: Your relationships are strained.

Is there someone in your life that you find difficult to talk to?

Chances are you may have some undelivered communication for them, or they with you, that's creating the chasm between you both.

Take a moment to reflect. If something comes up that you think may need communicating, I invite you to muster the courage to share it with this person to see if it causes a shift. If nothing comes up for you, consider asking them if they have something they've been holding onto that they'd like to share, and promise them you'll be open and receptive to hearing whatever it may be.

The level of happiness and fulfillment you'll experience in your life is largely determined by the quality of communication you have with those in your life.

If you suspect there may be some stuff that needs clearing up, take the time to flush it out, and chances are you'll find the person you've cleaned things up with will be far more interested in hearing about what else you'd like to create.

Sign #3: You have a hard time asking for what you want.

Asking for an upgrade at the airport or for a VIP table at the nicest restaurant in town (and getting it!) can be a fun way to enhance your experience in life to the fullest.

But are you comfortable asking for what it is that you desire?

When you're confident in your communication and authentic persuasion skills, you'll find that asking for what you want becomes easy - because when you ask, you very often get it! But if you find that you are hesitant to ask, you may still have some work to do to get more comfortable asserting your desires.

My recommendation is to start flexing your "ask" muscles by asking for smaller and simpler things, like signaling someone in traffic to see if they'll let you cut in, or asking a friend to meet you at your place instead of you meeting them at theirs. Practice makes perfect, so get cracking, and you'll soon feel more at ease asking for bigger and better things :)

Guest Chapter

By Joel Chue:[1]

Know Thyself and Increase Your Influence

Why knowing your strengths and weaknesses is a powerful force to influence and persuade in business, sales and life:

Introduction:

Knowing yourself can be divided into two types of relationships. The first and most obvious type is about how you relate to others (sometimes called the interpersonal relationship). The second less obvious type is about how you relate to yourself (sometimes called the intrapersonal relationship).

Interpersonal = knowing about and relating to others:

How you relate to others is the more obvious type of relationship because it is external and when people react to you, it affects you emotionally and your feelings are clearly impacted. It is easier for you to understand how you may have hurt someone else, how you may have made someone else angry – because they actually tell you what you have done. Either by

----

[1] Joel Chue is the co-creator of the iKnowThyself Brilliance Test. He has spent the last 10 years studying the influence of how your strengths and weaknesses is a powerful force to influence and persuade in business, sales and life. You can access the free iKnowThyself tool at: http://www.iKnowThyself.com

saying: "You've made me very angry" or by being angry with you and behaving in an angry manner towards you. So that you can learn about yourself and the influence you have on others by how others react to you. When you want to change the way you are and get better, you need to pre-empt this situation by maneuvering ahead of time to – in order to do this, you need to learn from experience and also look inside yourself.

Intrapersonal = knowing yourself and the emotional interplay going on inside of you:

How you relate to yourself from 'the inside' to 'the inside' as it were. This is much less obvious since it is an internal process and most of us rarely ask ourselves what is going on inside of us; what: 'makes us tick'. We are setting up an internal feedback loop. On a daily basis, we 'feel' emotions that provoke reactions and impulses inside of us - but we do not often take the time to analyse what is actually really going on inside: We do not stop to think how all of our inner emotions are interacting with each other, as we are feeling them, to produce a resulting attitude and/or behaviour. In order to progress with self-awareness, we need to stop and think carefully of these interactions.

Shifting our focal point from interpersonal to intrapersonal:

Because we tend to naturally focus on interpersonal relationships rather than on intrapersonal relationships, we use up a great deal of our energy focusing on what others are doing and how others are feeling and not on what we are feeling and on what our own inner needs are…Shifting the focal point from interpersonal to intrapersonal will give us a head start in investigating ourselves and learning who we really are. We will start to look at the inside as well as at the outside. Our own needs will become as important to us as the needs of others.

The iKnowthyself tool can help us to get closer to understanding our inner selves – in terms of how we feel about our relationships with others, to the world around us and how we feel about our relationships to ourselves. The tool asks us how we feel about certain situations in life. In turn, our feelings define our type of personality.

A) How not knowing yourself can create problems in the workplace:

As the introduction has shown, we spend a great deal of our time looking 'outside' of ourselves for points of reference – emotionally and also in the decision taking process. Indeed, we almost forget that we ourselves can also be responsible for 'driving' what is going on in our everyday lives at work and at play! We see and listen to others in our picture of the workplace and home, but some of us forget to include ourselves in what we see and who we listen to…Our lives become guided by our reactions to others rather than by what we really want deep down inside.

1) **How you appear to others - Body language:**

When we first apply for a job for example, we are highly conscious of the way we appear to our interviewer. We want to look our best – Over time however and as we settle into our role, this 'veneer' tends to lose its strength and we drop whatever image we were projecting with our best efforts to impress. As we get used to our job and surroundings, we become 'natural' – we start to say exactly what comes into our heads without thinking of the consequences, we may even start to act childishly or be overtly cynical about certain situations. This 'being natural' and acting impulsively may have some positive sides in our private lives – but it may not serve us quite so well in our work environment.

When at work, we have certain company/corporate objectives to pursue and we need to be fully conscious of those at all times, putting customer needs ahead of our own. We need to suspend our judgement and make every effort to operate in line with these objectives. Knowing ourselves may be a question of saying to ourselves: 'Hold your horses there, look at the bigger picture before opening your mouth…'

2) **Making other people feel a certain way by what you do and how you behave:**

Often we act certain ways without thinking that others are watching us and picking up cues from what we are doing. It may well be that we have reacted in a negative way to being asked to carry out a job by our manager. We may not even be conscious of our reaction – yet our manager, who has asked us to do the job, may well have picked up the 'vibe' that deep down inside we are reluctant to carry it out.

Perhaps we were very tense when we said: 'Yes that's fine'. Maybe we raised our voice defensively when asked about a detail that was not clear to our manager. If our manager then asks us to explain why we looked unhappy, it is then up to us to find the real reason for our anxiety. The fact is, we may not actually know the real reason ourselves! It may be so deep rooted and based on habit that it has escaped our attention.

There is nothing worst in a work environment than emotional undercurrents and tensions remaining unsaid and un-discussed. We then run the risk of developing toxic relationships with negative effects on work outcomes. These situation need to be nipped in the bud. Knowing ourselves better will help us to recognise when we are approaching this kind of misunderstanding and lack of healthy communication.

In these situations, it will always be helpful for us to understand who we really are.

The iKnowThyself tool will help us to do this. By knowing how we react to certain social/work situations, and whether we are more of an extrovert or more of an introvert, we can then go some way to explaining our reactions first to ourselves, and then to those around us.

B) Knowing your strengths and weaknesses can make you more effective and can create opportunities in the workplace:

1. **Knowing yourself can make you more effective by helping you to be more direct with others about what you want and what you need:**

If we are aware that we are a little shy and find it hard to express our inner thoughts to others without either feeling embarrassed or feeling that we might somehow be causing a conflict, then we can work on this weakness and make sure that we spend some time defining what we actually want and need from a given situation, before we are in that situation. There is no need to feel ashamed of what we want.

As long as we are not injuring anyone else, then we are perfectly entitled to having our own opinion about something and expressing reservations/disagreement if we feel that way. People will not be upset if they hear us speaking our mind, on the contrary, we are likely to gain their respect and possibly even their admiration.

2. **Finding common ground with others based on your strengths:**

Recently, Hilary Clinton mentioned in a radio interview how she was able to find common ground with President Putin of Russia. Putin, a man with whom she has very little in common apart from a great love of nature, got into a conversation with her about that aspect of their mutual interests. From that point onwards she said, they were able to build a working relationship despite all of their differences.

The lesson here is clear: In order to reach this kind of result, we need to share with others what we love and do well, then find out if they also have the same/similar passions and strengths. Then we can build on these.

Naturally, before really knowing what we love to do and what we do well, we sometimes need to do some research on ourselves using the tools at our disposal – one of these tools is: iKnowthyself.

3. **Avoiding working in areas where you are not so strong**

Once you have started to find out about your weaknesses, something quite incredible starts to happen, you actually start to feel stronger! It is paradoxical but true – knowing your weaknesses makes you stronger. This may well be because once you are aware of your weaknesses you can actually avoid working in areas where you know these weaknesses will be exposed. This does not mean that you live in permanent fear of making mistakes, quite the contrary, you are highly aware when those mistakes may happen and you are more able to manoeuvre your way around them.

Knowing ahead of time what people are likely to see as your weaknesses

When you know what people may identify as one of your less appealing character traits, then you can 'play that trait down'. You may want to try doing something that is completely 'counterintuitive' to you. For example, if you are used to simply accepting what people tell you to do without opposing them, you may want to try to stand up for yourself by explaining that you will not do something because you have other plans. As long as you can explain yourself logically and you have good reason to do what you are planning on doing, then there should really be no issue. Again, people are more likely to respect you for speaking your mind than to feel in any way negative about what you have shared with them.

4. **Being able to ask for help when you need it**

Finally, one of the most difficult things to do is to admit that you need help to get something done. This takes a significant amount of courage to do since you need to bypass your 'pride' and have the capacity to look at the bigger picture. You need to focus on achieving the objectives rather than on stubbornly proving that you are personally capable of performing a given task. If you are in the right kind of company, you will find that people, far from treating you in a negative way, will actually be grateful that you asked for help when you needed it.

Again iKnowthyself will help you to understand what kind of persons you are and where you may need a helping hand to achieve what you want.

C) How to influence based on your strengths and weaknesses:

1. **Knowing what is in your circles of Influence and Concern and distinguishing between what you can and cannot influence:**

Before you even start to look at influencing people, events and outcomes, you need to make sure you are attempting to influence something you actually can influence. In order to do this, you must think very carefully of what you care about and want to change and most of all, what is 'inside your circle of influence'. For example, you may care about the proliferation of nuclear weapons but not be able to do much about it, at least in the short to medium term. Nuclear weapon proliferation is a concern but may well be 'outside of your circle of influence'…However, you may also care about the results your child achieves in his end of year school examinations – this is clearly an outcome you can influence by your own attitude and actions. It is something which is 'inside your circle of influence'. You can act on it.

By operating within this circle of influence and changing the things you can actually change, you will increase your proactive approach and gradually, your circle of influence will widen and you will gain in confidence.

2. **Using your strengths to widen your circle of influence:**

Once you know your strengths from using the iKnowthyself tool, you can use these to widen your circle of influence. For example, if you enjoy being with others and going to parties, you are more than likely an extrovert and you will be able to promote your ideas or to sell certain products more easily than if you were shy and introverted.

3. Using your weaknesses to widen your circle of influence:

Being shy and introverted is often perceived as a weakness – yet if you know about this aspect of your personality, you may be in a better position to use it to your advantage. For example, you might want to try to work with people on a one to one basis rather than work with groups of people. You may also be in an ideal position to help others who are shy to understand how to overcome their shyness, since you know all about that yourself!

Again, iKnowthyself will help you to identify these so called 'weaknesses'. Once identified, you can find ways of working with them, rather than allowing them to hold you back and slow down your progress.

Final Thoughts

You now know how persuasion can be used to get your way in everyday situations. But don't just read this book once and leave it in your bookshelf for eternity. Re-read this book at least once every month until the concepts and ideas "sink in" to your subconscious.

And of course, knowing is different from actual application. It's not enough to know, but you have to apply your knowledge in the real world as often as you can. Only then will you truly experience its remarkable benefits.

Always remember to use persuasion ethically - not only for your own good but also for everyone else's. We should always aim to get what we want in a win-win situation. Everyone involved in the persuasion process should feel that they have benefited in some way - or at least feel that they haven't lost anything. As said in the Spiderman movie, "With great power comes great responsibility."

Have an awesome time persuading!

From the Author

Check out my site for free gifts, updates, and interesting info:
- Author Blog – www.expertpersuader.com

If you enjoyed any of my books then please share the love and write a review for the book.

If you have questions or comments then feel free to email me. (Just know that these emails are filtered by my publisher.)

Good news is always welcome.

One Last Thing, For Kindle Readers...

When you turn the page after the bibliography, Kindle will give you the opportunity to rate this book and share your thoughts on Facebook and Twitter. If you enjoyed my writings, would you please take a few seconds to let your friends know about it? Because... when they enjoy they will be grateful to you and so will I.

Thank You!

Michael Lee
michael_lee@awesomeauthors.org

Bibliography

Barron, David R. and Danek S. Kaus. *Power Persuasion: Using Hypnotic Influence To Win In Life, Love, And Business.* Bandon, OR: Robert D. Reed Publishers, 2005.

Boothman, Nicholas. *Convince Them In 90 Seconds: Make Instant Connections That Pay Off In Business And In Life.* New York, Workman Publishing, 2002, 2010.

Byrne, Rhonda. *The Secret.* New York: Atria Books, 2006.

Cialdini, Robert B. *Influence: The Psychology Of Persuasion.* New York: William Morrow & Company, 1984, 1993.

Dawson, Roger. *Secrets Of Power Persuasion.* New York: Prentice-Hall, 1992.

Goldstein, Noah with Steve J. Martin and Robert B. Cialdini. *Yes! 50 Scientifically Proven Ways To Be Persuasive.* New York: Free Press, 2008.

Hogan, Kevin and James Speakman. *Covert Persuasion: Psychological Tactics And Tricks To Win The Game.* Hoboken, NJ: John Wiley & Sons, 2006.

Hogan, Kevin and Mary Lee Labay. *Irresistible Attraction: Secrets Of Personal Magnetism.* Eagan, MN: Network 3000 Publishing, 2000.

Hogan, Kevin. *The Psychology Of Persuasion: How To Persuade Others To Your Way Of Thinking.* Gretna, LA: Pelican Publishing, 1996.

Lakhani, Dave. *Persuasion: The Art Of Getting What You Want.* Hoboken, NJ: John Wiley & Sons, 2005.

Levine, Robert. *The Power Of Persuasion: How We're Bought And Sold.* Hoboken, NJ: John Wiley & Sons, 2003.

Lieberman, David J. *Get Anyone To Do Anything.* New York: St. Martin's Griffin, 2000.

Lieberman, David J. How To Change Anybody. New York: St. Martin's Griffin, 2005.

Lieberman, David J. *Never Be Lied To Again*. New York: St. Martin's Griffin, 1998.

Lowndes, Leil. *How To Talk To Anyone*. New York: Mc Graw Hill, 2003.

Maltz, Maxwell. *Psycho-Cybernetics*. New York: Pocket Books, 1960

Mortensen, Kurt W. *Maximum Influence: The 12 Universal Laws Of Power Persuasion*. New York: AMACOM, 2004.

Navarro, Joe and Marvin Karlins. *What Every Body Is Saying*. New York: Harper Collins Publishers, 2008.

Nierenberg, Gerald I. and Henry H. Calero. *How To Read A Person Like A Book*. New York: Pocket Books, 1971.

Puhn, Laurie. *Instant Persuasion: How To Change Your Words To Change Your Life*. New   York: Penguin Group, 2005

Robbins, Anthony. *Unlimited Power*. New York: Free Press, 1986.

Sanders, Tim. *The Likeability Factor*. New York: Crown Publishing, 2005.

Schwartz, Dr. David J. *The Magic Of Thinking Big*. New York: Prentice-Hall, 1959, 1965.

Smith, Manuel J. *When I Say No, I Feel Guilty*. New York: Bantam Books, 1975

Tutt, Alan. *Choose To Believe*. Grand Rapids, MI: PowerKeys Publishing, 2008.

Tutt, Alan. *Keys To Power Persuasion*. Grand Rapids, MI: PowerKeys Publishing, 2006.

22144667R00118

Printed in Great Britain
by Amazon